RECORD-BREAKERS
of the Major Leagues

Fifteen exciting accounts of modern baseball
stars who got their names in the record book.

RECORD-BREAKERS
of the Major Leagues

BY LOU SABIN

illustrated with photographs

Random House · New York

MAJOR LEAGUE
LIBRARY

PHOTOGRAPH CREDITS: Clifton Boutelle: 52, 74; Malcolm Emmons: 6, 14, 37, 61, 95, 128, 142; Ken Regan (Camera Five): 134–135; Fred Roe: 2–3; United Press International: endpapers, 16, 28, 41, 47, 57, 74, 75, 79, 86, 90, 92, 99, 106, 111, 116, 119, 124, 131, 144–145; Wide World Photos: 19, 24, 27, 32, 45, 66, 69, 102, 109, 139.
Cover: photo by Tony Triolo SPORTS ILLUSTRATED © Time Inc.

Library of Congress Cataloging in Publication Data
Sabin, Louis.   Record-breakers of the major leagues.   (Major league library)
SUMMARY: Traces the careers of baseball players who have broken major league records.   1.   Baseball—Biography—Juvenile literature.
[1.   Baseball—Biography]   I.   Title.
GV865.A1S22   1974   796.357′092′2[B]   [920]   73-18740
ISBN 0-394-82769-4   ISBN 0-394-92769-9 (lib. bdg.)

to

Keith

who holds the record as World's Greatest Son

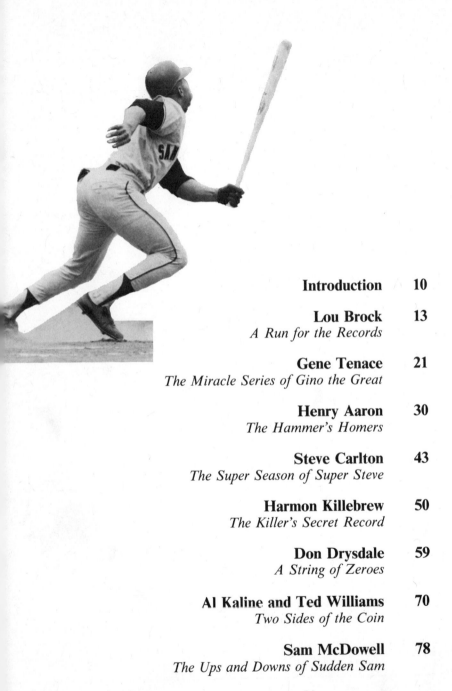

Contents

RECORD-BREAKERS
of the Major Leagues

Introduction

Records are the heart and soul of baseball. In over 100 years of major-league history, a long list of remarkable records have been written—and rewritten—by the game's hard-throwing, hard-hitting and hard-running superheroes.

Some of those records seem just about unbreakable— Ty Cobb's .367 lifetime batting average, for instance, or Joe Dimaggio's 56-game hitting streak, or Cy Young's 511 pitching victories.

But who can say that any record is unbreakable? Babe Ruth's 714 home runs seemed way out of reach— until Hammerin' Hank Aaron came along to attack them with his big bat. Ty Cobb's record of 96 stolen bases in one season was in the book for 50 years until Maury Wills came along. And Rube Waddell's 349 strikeouts in one season were unsurpassed for 60 years before Sandy Koufax racked up 382 in 1965. But even that record fell when Nolan Ryan whiffed 383 in 1973.

This book is about the breaking of records and the men who broke them. Here you'll read about super-hurlers like Tom Seaver, Steve Carlton, Bob Gibson and Don Drysdale; batting champs like Henry Aaron, Willie Mays and Ted Williams; and champion base-stealer Lou Brock.

There are even some records that players try *not* to break, and you'll read about those, too. There's the pitcher who gave up the most walks, the hitter who had the most major league strikeouts, and a player who held the painful record of being hit most often by pitched balls.

Hitting, pitching, fielding, base-running. It's all here. By the time you've finished *Record-Breakers of the Major Leagues*, you'll know a lot more about the grand old game of baseball. You'll also know why baseball fans say over and over again, "Records are made to be broken."

Lou Brock

A Run for the Records

The saying "Records are made to be broken" holds true even for those marks baseball buffs consider "unreachable." Yet Roger Maris and Hank Aaron came along to break two of Babe Ruth's unreachable home-run records. And Maury Wills snapped the great Ty Cobb's single-season high of 96 stolen bases by stealing 104 in 1962. Then along came Lou Brock, who proved once again that even the immortal Cobb set records that could be broken.

Even standing still, 5-foot-11, 175-pound Louis Clark Brock looked fast. On the basepaths he *was* fast. Dancing away from first or second, with a pitcher squinting nervously over his shoulder, he was a living definition of lightning ready to strike, and sprinting from base to base, he moved with a swiftness that made every other action seem slow by comparison.

Faster than you can say "Lou Brock," the St. Louis speedster is on his way to first base.

Everyone loved to see Brock go—everyone but the opposing team, that is. Larry Jackson was one of many pitchers who hated to see Brock get on base. "It seems that Brock is in on four out of every five Cardinal rallies," Jackson moaned. "He puts the heat on the defense. He puts the heat on the pitcher and the outfield and catcher, too, because they know they have to hurry plays when he's on base."

That was just the kind of fearful thinking Brock worked for. More than anything else, he wanted to paralyze the heads and hearts of every player on the other team. He was convinced that their fears were more important than his speed. "Speed isn't all-important," Lou insisted. "I've played with plenty of guys who were faster than I was yet couldn't run the bases. The element of surprise is overrated, too. If I was the kind of runner who depended on surprise, I'd steal no more than 25 or 30 bases a year. Speed is a tool; surprise is a tactic. The *art* of base-running is knowing when and if to use them.

"When I get on base, no matter what the situation, I always have the same things in mind. I am thinking about the catcher's strengths and limitations. I am 'reading' the pitcher, looking for some clue in his style that will tell me when I can run. Meanwhile, they're reading me. The pitcher knows I'm gonna go, the catcher knows, the fans know. And that's one of the keys to successful base stealing: making them aware that I'm a threat. Because once I have them trying to make the perfect play to stop me, I've beaten them. The more they try to shoot for perfection, the more likely they'll make an error. So base-running isn't just speed or surprise. It's forcing the opposition into errors."

It was that kind of big-league savvy that carried Lou past the 600 mark in stolen bases during the 1973 season. And it was that kind of winning baseball that prompted Red Schoendienst, his manager on the St. Louis Cardinals, to declare, "What is there he can't do? He can hit with power. He can steal. He can take the extra base and turn singles into doubles. He *has* to be the most exciting player in the National League."

There was nothing very exciting about Lou's first full season for the Chicago Cubs in 1963. In fact, his fielding

It's a close call, but Brock is out at second on an attempted steal.

was poor, his hitting was no better than fair and he stole just 16 bases. And even though he increased his basepath thievery to 24 the next year, Brock still wasn't showing enough all-around skills to look like much of a prospect. So the Cubs traded him to the Cardinals late in 1964—and were sorry ever after.

"I decided to forget trying to be a long-ball hitter," Brock said after the trade. "Instead, I concentrated on getting on base and stealing."

Brock's concentration paid off. Not only did his fielding improve, but his batting average leaped over the .300 level for the first time in his major-league career. He added a satisfying ending to the 1964 season with a .315 batting mark and 43 stolen bases. Lou Brock was off and running, and absolutely nobody was going to stop him.

There were more .300-plus seasons ahead, as Brock became a fixture in left field and the leadoff slot in the St. Louis batting order. But the real excitement came from his flying spikes. From 1965 through 1972 the St. Louis swifty stole bases at a fantastic rate. In 1965 he had 63 stolen bases, and he followed that with a glittering total of 74 in 1966. Then he flew on to record 52 SB's in '67, 62 in '68 (when he led the NL in doubles, triples and stolen bases), 53 in '69, 51 in '70, 64 in '71 and 63 in '72. That brought his eleven-year career mark to 565 stolen bases. And in 1973, at the advanced baseball age of 34, he zoomed through the 600 barrier with 70 more.

Running or hitting, Brock constantly outdid himself when his team needed him most. Like great players in all sports, he was always "up for the big ones." The 1967

World Series was a perfect example of Lou Brock at his best. He started the opening game against the Boston Red Sox by singling, then stealing second on the first pitch to the next batter. In that game he delivered four hits in four times at bat, and that was just the beginning. Lou's hot bat hammered out a .414 average for the entire Series, with 12 hits in 29 at-bats. And he stole seven bases to set a new record for a seven-game Series.

It hardly seemed fair to expect Brock to match his 1967 heroics when the Cardinals took on the Detroit Tigers in the 1968 World Series—but that's just what he did. Lou not only equalled his freshly minted record of seven steals in a seven-game Series, but he batted a rousing .464, including three doubles, one triple and two home runs. His 1968 Series accumulation of 24 total bases tied a record that had endured for 16 years; his six extra-base hits tied another mark; his 13 total hits tied another; and his eight runs scored tied still another.

As much as Lou's hitting thrilled the fans, it was clearly his base-running that brought them up cheering. "People are beginning to believe that Brock is ten feet tall," wrote one sports columnist, "and that he can run the 90 feet between the bases in nothing flat."

By the end of 1972 he had hustled his way right into the record books, on the same line as Ty Cobb, by notching his eighth season of 50 or more stolen bases. Those 50-plus seasons also happened to be consecutive, a feat that put him in a class by himself. He had outdistanced Cobb by a country mile, since the best the Georgia Peach could manage was five consecutive years of 50 or more, back in 1909–13.

Another measure of Brock's running superiority is

Lou reaches second with his fourth stolen base of the 1967 World Series.

that he succeeded three out of every four times he took off for the next base. There weren't many runners in the game's long history who could work that kind of magic. And there were even fewer who had his kind of speed at his age. Already in his mid-30s, Brock began the 1973 season with a goal of at least another 50 stolen bases. That number would give him nine consecutive seasons of 50-plus, an improvement over his own top line in the record book. More important, they would also give him full ownership of the most-seasons-of-50-or-more stolen bases he shared with Cobb.

Did he make it? Of course he did. On August 26, against the Cincinnati Reds, Brock stole his 50th base of the season—and took his place as the most consistent base stealer in history. He finished the season with 70, boosting his career total to 635. No one could stop the thief who had stolen his way into the hearts of millions of fans.

Gene Tenace

The Miracle Series of Gino the Great

Any time talk turns to World Series slugging stars, certain names spring to mind. Mickey Mantle, Duke Snider, Babe Ruth, Gene Tenace . . .

Gene *who?* Have you already forgotten the hero of the 1972 World Series? He was the man whose bat so dominated those championship games that fans hardly noticed the other more famous sluggers.

Sal Bando was there. He was one of Tenace's teammates on the Oakland Athletics, and many people expected Sal to lead the Series in four-baggers. And if he didn't do it, the rival Cincinnati Reds fans were certain Johnny Bench would. In fact, Cincinnati rooters insisted that Bench and his teammate Tony Perez were sure-fire candidates to pulverize the A's pitching staff. As for Fiore Gino Tenace, there was some doubt that he would even appear in the line-up.

Oakland manager Dick Williams could have used Tenace at first base, but that would have meant benching Mike Epstein, an iron-muscled swinger with the proven ability to slug a baseball out of sight. Williams could have put Tenace behind the plate, but that would mean keeping first-string catcher Dave Duncan out of the line-up. There was also the possibility of starting Tenace in the outfield, but the A's were set out there.

Considering Gene's past performances, there really wasn't much reason to use him in the all-important Series. In 227 at-bats Gene had hit a meager .225, with only 32 RBI's and five home runs. Comparing home run production alone, Tenace didn't even come close to Joe Rudi's 19, Bando's 15, or Duncan's 19. The only evidence that Tenace could hit the long ball came from his minor-league statistics. And even those weren't particularly impressive. Gene had hit 21 homers back in 1968, but that was in the lowly Carolina League. Tenace not only lacked the credentials of a potential hero, he hardly qualified as a starter.

There was only one real argument in favor of starting Tenace. Neither Duncan nor Epstein had been hitting well at the end of the season, and Duncan particularly was in a batting slump. So, almost as if choosing the lesser of two evils, manager Williams decided to go with Tenace as his catcher for the Series opener.

As he knelt in the on-deck circle at Cincinnati's Riverfront Stadium in the second inning, Tenace watched teammate George Hendrick draw a base on balls from Cincinnati pitcher Gary Nolan. Then Tenace moved in to bat with two out and no score. The pitcher staring down at him had just finished a fine year with 15 wins against 5 losses, and he had allowed only two home runs in all of 1972.

Nolan took the sign from Johnny Bench and came in with a high fastball. Tenace put all the power of his 6-foot, 190-pound body behind the swing and belted the ball over the left-field fence. Bang! Just like that, Oakland had a 2–0 lead, and Tenace had the distinction of tying a World Series record by hitting a home run in his first plate appearance. If he did nothing more for the rest of his baseball career, Gene Tenace was permanently in the record book.

The Reds answered with a run in their half of the second and another in the fourth to even the score at 2–2. Nolan had settled down after the shock of Tenace's blow, giving up only a single to Bert Campaneris. When the A's catcher stepped into the batter's box with nobody on base in the top of the fifth, Nolan was ready for him—or so he thought. Having been stung by Gene on a fastball the first time, the Cincinnati pitcher fed him a curve. But it hung, as Nolan later described it, "like a feather." Tenace leaned right into it. The ball sailed down the left-field line and landed in the upper deck for another home run.

Tenace stood frozen at the plate, following the flight of the ball. "I wasn't showing off," he assured reporters after the game. "I just wasn't sure the ball would stay fair, and I wanted to help it all I could."

As he completed his triumphant tour of the bases, Tenace moved out of mediocrity and into the record books. He was now in a class by himself—the only man ever to hit home runs in his first two World Series

Oakland's Gene Tenace blasts his first homer of the 1972 World Series.

at-bats. Gene's four-bagger also moved Oakland back in front, and that's the way the contest ended: Tenace 3–Cincinnati 2.

The second game brought another Oakland victory over the heavily favored Reds in their own ballpark. But Tenace's bat was silent in this one, a squeaker that ended with Oakland on top, 2–1.

Witnesses who had watched many a Series were sure that Gene's two-homer outburst had been a freak. No one expected any further dramatics from Tenace as the third game got underway in Oakland. And they were right in this instance. He went 0–for–3 in the A's 1–0 loss to the Reds. In fact, fans were wondering if Gene would even get to play in the next game. But there he was, still behind the plate, as the Reds met the A's in the Oakland Coliseum for game four.

It was another pitchers' duel that didn't see a run scored until the bottom of the fifth inning. Don Gullett, Cincy's fastballing southpaw, had been keeping a tight rein on the Oakland hitters when the fast-fading Tenace came up for his second time at bat. The right-handed hitter hadn't picked up even a single in his last nine appearances. Here, however, was a chance to recapture the spotlight with a big hit. And right on cue, Gene Tenace leaped right back into the spotlight by hammering a Gullett pitch into the hands of scrambling fans in the left-field seats. This time Tenace didn't dally at home plate. He was halfway to first when the ball left the playing field.

For a while it looked as if Gene's third homer of the Series would hold up as the winning run. But Cincinnati scored twice in the top of the eighth, and the Athletics failed to get a run in their half of the inning.

The Reds didn't add anything in the top of the ninth, and the A's came up for their last licks. The game stood Cincinnati 2–Oakland 1. One out, bases empty. Then Oakland pinch-hitter Gonzalo Marquez bounced a single through the middle off reliever Pedro Borbon. Enter the homer-happy hero, Gene Tenace. Can he do it again? The answer comes swiftly: no. He "only" slashes a single between short and third, starting a rally that makes it possible for two other A's to share the spotlight with him.

One is Don Mincher, who pops a single into right-center field, scoring Marquez with the game-tying run. The second is Angel Mangual, who delivers another single that sends Tenace scampering home with the winning run. He crosses the plate and, star that he is, tips his hat to the applauding audience.

On stage for game five, Tenace blasted another one into the stands. And suddenly it wasn't merely a star performance, it was practically a one-man show. By slugging his fourth World Series home run, Gino the Great had matched bats with Babe Ruth, Duke Snider and Hank Bauer, the only others to bang out that many round-trippers in a single Series.

What did it matter that the A's lost the game, 5–4? Or that they lost the next one, 8–1, with Tenace collecting just one single in four at-bats? The Series was tied at three games apiece. There was still the last one to come—the perfect finish to a dramatic seven-act play. It was the ideal setting for Gene Tenace to complete his miracle play with an encore that would bring down the house.

Tenace does it again with his fourth home run of the Series.

And sure enough, when the curtain closed, the
Athletics had taken their final bows as world champions
with a 3–2 victory. And what part did Tenace play in
this? There was no crowd-tingling home run from the
bat of Tenace the Menace this time. Instead, there was a
single and a double in three trips to the plate. The single

Back in the dugout, Gino the Great is surrounded by his happy teammates.

drove in Oakland's first run in the opening inning, and the double drove in Oakland's last—and winning—run in the top of the sixth. The final score was 3–2, Oakland, and the indisputable superstar was Gene Tenace. Now everyone knew Gene *who!*

When all the post-Series adding and dividing was done, the keepers of the record books found that not only had Tenace set new milestones with his home runs, he had powered past the mightiest hitter of them all, George Herman Ruth. Until 1972, the highest slugging average for a seven-game Series was the Babe's .900. No more—Gene had established the new high with a .913 slugging percentage.

Naturally, Tenace was voted the Most Valuable Player of the 1972 World Series. In addition to those four homers, he had batted .348 and driven in nine of Oakland's 16 runs. No one expected Gene Tenace to go after all the other records of Babe Ruth. But for seven crucial games he outdid the Babe and everyone else. As the record books will show, Gene's 1972 Series was simply incomparable.

Henry Aaron

The Hammer's Homers

The Atlanta Braves' Number 44 gripped the bat and settled into his batting stance. He looked as relaxed as if he were watching the game in the comfort of his living room. But no other player on the field was relaxed, nor were the 5,119 fans in Atlanta Stadium. It was September 2, 1972—a big day in the baseball life of Henry Aaron.

Leading off third base was Sonny Jackson, who had just tripled in a run for the Braves in the bottom of the first. The Philadelphia Phillies had scored five times in the top of the inning, however, so Atlanta still had some catching up to do.

"Come on, Henry," Jackson shouted to the 6-foot, 180-pound batter. "Bring me home."

Aaron nodded slightly and got ready for Darrell Brandon's pitch. The Philly hurler wound up, checked

Jackson at third, reared back and snapped a curve toward the plate. With perfect timing, Aaron whipped his bat around. *Crack!* The ball soared toward left field and came down in the stands.

The crowd roared as Jackson scored, then turned to watch Aaron circle the bases. That home run had brought Atlanta within two runs of Philadelphia. It had also brought Henry Aaron closer to a new major-league record. Now Hammerin' Hank, with his 666th home run adding another four bases to his lifetime total, was just four short of Stan Musial's mark of 6,134 total career bases.

In his next two at-bats Aaron failed to get a hit. When he strode to the plate in the seventh inning, the Braves were trailing the Phillies, 7–4. Hank squared off against right-handed relief pitcher Dick Selma. He fouled off Selma's first pitch, and took the second for a ball. The next pitch was a fastball, just above the knees. Hank teed off and the ball took off like a rocket. The fans leaped to their feet to watch, as its downward flight carried it into a sea of waiting hands in the left-field seats.

Hank Aaron's 667th career home run had tied him with Musial for the record of most total bases in a career. It also sparked a five-run uprising that ended in a 10–7 Braves victory.

The next day Hank faced the Phillies' ace left-hander, Steve Carlton. Carlton was having a great season, one that would put his name into the record books, too. But not even he could stop Hank from collecting a single in his first at-bat, the hit that carried Aaron past Musial to the top of the list for career total bases: 6,135. By the

Hank Aaron lifts his cap to the cheering crowd after another big homer.

time the 1972 season was over, Hank had upped his pace-setting figure to 6,172. And there were many more to come.

The Hank Aaron of 1972 was, in many ways, much like the Hank Aaron of 1951. Back then, at the age of 17, he weighed only 10 pounds less than he would in the last years of his career. His slender build only hinted at the strength he could put into a throw or swing. What impressed people most was the stunning power of young Hank's wrists. They could whip a bat around so swiftly that it seemed a man twice his size was taking the cut.

At 17, Hank was the same relaxed batter he remained throughout his playing days. He showed none of the tension and determination, in face or body, that characterized such fierce competitors as Ted Williams. Nor did he display any of the menacing practice swings or grim expressions other sluggers used to warn a pitcher that they were going to crush any ball near the plate. Hank simply got ready in his cool, calm way and patiently waited for the ball to get within reach. His bat did the rest.

In 1951, Aaron was hitting for average and distance, while playing shortstop for the Indianapolis Clowns of the American Black Baseball League. Yet, as well as he hit, there was something very strange about the way he batted. As a right-handed swinger, his left hand should have been higher on the bat handle than his right hand. But Henry's pose was just the opposite—his right hand was over his left. He also hit off the wrong foot. Instead of taking his cuts with his weight centered on his right foot (the foot near the catcher, which should be acting as an anchor to supply power and balance), he leaned forward and threw his weight on the front foot. To top it all off, he would drop the bat slightly as he started to bring it around on a pitch. That "hitch" in his stroke prevented him from swinging on a level, the way all young players are taught to bat.

Hank's manager with the Clowns helped him break the habit of swinging cross-handed—or thought he did. But years later Aaron admitted that he "cheated" once in a while. "If the pitcher had two strikes on me and my manager was in the third-base dugout, so he couldn't see, I'd slip the bottom hand on top," he confessed.

By 1952, however, Hank had given up the habit of hitting cross-handed. He was playing for the Braves' Eau Claire farm team then, and he had his eyes on the majors. Even though he continued to hit off the wrong foot and still had a hitch in his swing, nobody had any complaints. Hank Aaron was obviously doing something right! He batted .336 for Eau Claire and in 1953 was moved up to Jacksonville, a Florida farm team of the Braves. Hank's glovework at shortstop was producing too many errors, making it clear that he was better suited for the outfield. But his batwork was something else. He led the South Atlantic (Sally) League with a .362 batting average, 125 runs batted in, 208 hits and 115 runs scored. At the age of 19, Henry Aaron was voted the league's Most Valuable Player. The following season he began a major-league career that would see an endless barrage of Hank-hammered baseballs flying out of National League stadiums for years to come.

As a 20-year-old rookie in 1954, Henry became a regular in the Braves outfield. By that time he had corrected almost all of his batting flaws. The only "problem" that remained was that he still hit off his left foot. However, it wasn't a problem to Hank, only to opposing pitchers. Years after he had become one of baseball's greatest sluggers, Aaron explained: "I know most guys couldn't hit the way I do, so I'm lucky that what I have to do comes naturally. But that isn't all there is to it. My weight is forward as I swing, but my hands are back, so the bat can't get fooled."

It took the rookie two weeks to hit his first home run, on April 23, 1953, and he finished the season with 13. He also batted .280 and drove in 69 runs. The next year he really started steaming, producing 27 homers, a .314 batting average and 105 RBI's. He also scored 105 times, an important statistic since a man's value to his team must be measured by more than just his personal records.

He soon earned the reputation of a quiet, efficient slugger. Not only was he a fearsome hitter, he was also the kind of player who put all his talents to work for the good of the team. Bobby Bragan, one of Hank's managers on the Braves, praised Aaron by saying, "If you need a stolen base, Henry will steal it, quietly. If you need a shoestring catch, he'll make it, and his cap won't come flying off. And if you need a hit, he's there to get it."

Bragan was indirectly comparing Aaron to Willie Mays, whose flamboyant style of losing his cap while catching fly balls and running the bases won him far more fame and nationwide popularity than Hank. But if his own lack of publicity bothered Aaron, he kept it to himself.

In 1956, Henry tacked another 26 home runs onto his young career total, drove in 92 runs and hit .328, the best batting average in the National League that season. The *Sporting News* honored him as its National League Player of the Year.

It was in 1957, however, that Hammerin' Hank really hit the stride he would maintain for the rest of his career. He took the league's home-run title by blasting 44. The last one, a grand-slammer, came in the final game of the season. It raised his season's batting average to .322 and his league-leading RBI total to 132. All this earned him the National League's Most Valuable Player award. But the MVP title wasn't nearly as important to Hank as the fact that the Braves won the NL pennant, then went on to beat the Yankees in the World Series.

One of the high points in his baseball career came in the game that clinched the NL flag. In the bottom of the eleventh inning, the score was tied at 2–2. With two out and a man on first, Hammerin' Hank came up to bat. One moment the Braves' slugger was settling into his deceptively relaxed batting stance, the next moment he was uncoiling his powerhouse swing as a pitch from Billy Muffett came spinning toward the plate. Bat met ball, and the explosive strength of Aaron's wrists and forearms sent it whizzing back. A blur of white, the baseball didn't stop until it had cleared the center-field fence and slammed to earth—402 feet from home plate. The Braves had won the 1957 pennant.

"It was the biggest thrill of my career," Hank said after the games. "The first thing I thought about was Bobby Thomson's homer, the one that won the 1951

Even Hank doesn't always hit home runs. Here he eyes a pop-up fly.

pennant for the Giants. That's always been my idea of the most important homer. Now I got one for myself. I mean, for *me* to get the hit myself. Am I excited!"

A Henry Aaron home run could have been expected. What really surprised writers and fans was the bubbling exuberance of this man who had a well-known reputation for being soft-spoken and unemotional. It was that reserved manner, both on the field and off, that had kept him out of the limelight. But it was just a matter of time before his all-around greatness would make it impossible to focus the spotlight anywhere but on Hank Aaron.

In 1958, Aaron led the Braves to another pennant. And in 1959 he again captured the batting crown, with a .355 average. Things got even better in the 1960s. In 1963, and again in '66, he tied Willie McCovey for the home-run leadership, walloping 44 four-baggers each year. And in 1967, Aaron claimed the title for himself, with 39 round-trippers. The next year he slammed the 500th homer of his career. In 1969 he hit 44 more, just one less than McCovey's league-leading 45.

As homer followed homer, Henry moved steadily up the all-time home-run list. As the years went by, he climbed past Mel Ott's 511, Eddie Matthews' 512, Ted Williams' 521, Jimmy Foxx's 534 and Mickey Mantle's 536. Finally, only one man, Willie Mays, stood between Hank and Babe Ruth's magical 714 record. And while it was clear that Mays was slowing down, Henry Aaron was still speeding along in high gear.

In 1970 the 36-year-old Aaron banged 38 baseballs out of the park. The next season saw him club 47 more, as he passed the 600 mark. That was enough to insure baseball immortality for Hammerin' Hank. But he also showed excellence—and set records—in a number of other departments. By 1972 he had blasted his name into the record books in several slugging categories.

His most memorable hit of that season came on June 24 during a game against the Phillies before 23,242 Philadelphia fans. Henry was 0–for–2 when the sixth inning started. The Braves' shortstop, Marty Perez, opened with a walk off right-hander Wayne Twitchell. Atlanta pitcher Tom Kelley laid down a sacrifice bunt and was safe when Twitchell threw wildly to first. Twitchell got the next two batters out, but a walk to outfielder Ralph Garr filled the bases with Braves.

Up stepped the last man Twitchell wanted to face with the bases loaded—Henry Aaron. Aaron didn't take long to show why pitchers all over the league called him Bad Henry. He picked out a serve from Twitchell and drove it high and far.

The three Braves on base watched it disappear, then dented the plate ahead of him. As Henry crossed home his teammates poured out of the dugout to shake his hand and slap his back. With that one home run Hank had picked up two big records. As the 14th grand slam of his career, it tied Gil Hodges' National League record. But even more important, as his 649th homer, it swept him past Willie Mays and into second place on the all-time home-run list.

Asked how he felt about this, Aaron said, "I have no rivalry going with Willie. The big one is still ahead." It wasn't Willie he wanted, it was the Babe himself!

Although he had not seriously thought about setting records early in his career, Henry admitted he was becoming more record-conscious as his career reached its finest moments. While he knew that Lou Gehrig's mark of 23 lifetime grand slams was well out of his reach, Aaron had already broken a record of Gehrig's that had been in the books since 1938. Until Hank came along, Gehrig's feat of scoring 100 or more runs in 13 seasons was the high-water mark in that department. Aaron equalled that number in 1967, then raced beyond it in '69 and '70, establishing the all-time scoring record of 100 or more runs in 15 seasons.

Still another remarkable record chalked up by Hammerin' Hank was his National League mark of most career RBI's. He had driven home 2,133 when the 1973 season ended. The only man in baseball history with more RBI's to his credit was Babe Ruth, with 2,216.

Another one for the books—and this one *did* erase a record set by the Babe—was set by Aaron on September 13, 1972. In a game against the Cincinnati Reds, Aaron powered his 30th homer of the season. It was the 14th year he had hit 30 or more four-baggers, and it topped Ruth's record total of 13 years with 30 or more homers.

However, it had been two years earlier, in 1970, that Aaron created a brand-new record that had eluded not only George Herman Ruth but every other slugger to play the game. On May 17 of that year, Hammerin' Hank tagged Cincinnati right-hander Wayne Simpson for an infield single in the first game of a doubleheader. It may not have looked like an important hit, but it was the 3,000th one of Hank's career and, coupled with his more than 500 home runs, made him the only player ever to combine those two achievements in one career.

On July 21, 1973, Aaron hammers out his 700th career home run.

"I wasn't too happy with that single," Aaron said after the second game. "I wanted hit number 3,000 to be a clean one. When I got a homer in the next game, I felt much better."

Game after game, season after season, Henry Aaron pounded the ball with ferocious consistency. And as the runs and hits continued to mount, "the old man with the young body" wondered just how far he could go before hanging up his spikes. "Some days I feel like going for the records," he said, thinking about the ones he had set and the ones still to come, "and some days I don't."

His 34 homers in 1972 brought Hank's total to 673. Yet it wasn't until he was well into the 1973 season, with Ruth's "unreachable" homer mark coming closer and closer, that the 39-year-old slugger told reporters that home run number 715 was the hit he wanted most of all. It was the big one, the crown to top off a royal career.

So Henry hammered away, rocketing 40 four-baggers over the 1973 season. That brought his total to 713, tantalizingly close to the magic number. But the big one, and the ones to follow, wouldn't come until 1974. It was worth waiting for!

Steve Carlton

The Super Season of Super Steve

Southpaw Steve Carlton's pitching arm was doing funny things on the night of September 15, 1969. When he was good, he was very, very good. But when he was bad—ugh! The New York Mets, swinging away at his mixed bag of pitches, were having uneven results against the St. Louis Cardinal hurler. By the time the nine-inning contest was history, Carlton had lost the game—but made some history of his own. It was enough to make a man laugh and cry in the same breath.

Carlton could laugh because he had struck out 19 Mets, breaking the major-league record of 18 that had been shared by Sandy Koufax, Bob Feller and Don Wilson. "I had a fever all day," Carlton said after his 19-strikeout beauty, "and I felt so bad that I slept an extra hour and didn't get to the ballpark until seven o'clock, an hour before the game was to start. But it was the best stuff I ever had."

Nevertheless, when they weren't flailing helplessly at his offerings, the Mets were able to zero in on Steve's "best stuff" often enough to down the Redbirds, 4–3—no laughing matter. New York outfielder Ron Swoboda, the slugging hero of the night, was an ideal example of the Mets' do-or-die batsmanship. After being whiffed twice by Carlton, Swoboda did an about-face by clobbering Steve for a pair of home runs.

"He'd throw a pitch so good," Swoboda said, "that I'd say to myself, 'If he throws two more like it, there's no way I can touch him.'" Nevertheless, Swoboda did get hold of a couple that were extremely touchable.

In some ways that game was a typical one for the 6-foot-5, 195-pound hurler. The pitching career of Stephen N. Carlton can most truly be described as hot and cold. In 1967, his first full season with the St. Louis Cardinals, Steve won 14 and lost 9. In '68 he had 13 wins and 11 losses. He did better in 1969, with 17 wins against 11 losses and a fine earned run average of 2.17. But in 1970, Steve reversed his form and wound up with a dismal 10 victories, 19 defeats and a 3.72 ERA. Then, consistently inconsistent, he surged back in '71 with his first 20-win season, logging a 20–9 record despite a 3.56 ERA.

On the strength of those 20 wins, Carlton demanded a sizable salary increase from Cardinal owner Gussie Busch. Busch, a wealthy beer tycoon, reminded Carlton of his 19 losses in '70. Carlton countered with his 20 wins in '71. But Busch had the last word, trading Steve to the Philadelphia Phillies for Rick Wise.

Steve Carlton winds up for his record-setting 19th strikeout in a 1969 game against the New York Mets.

When Steve joined the Phillies in 1972 he found a sad lot of ballplayers. By the end of the season, it wasn't hard to see why they were in the National League East cellar. Greg Luzinski, the team's best hitter, had earned that designation with a .281 batting average and 18 home runs. Fair—but hardly the kind of statistics a manager wants to see at the top of his list. As a team, the Phillies had batted a dismal .236, and their won–lost record was a depressing 59–97.

Steve Carlton, however, shone like a pearl in a sea of mud. That same year he won 27 games and lost only 10. Of the total 59 games won by the Phillies, his 27 victories made up almost half of those wins—45.8 percent, to be exact. He surrendered a slim average of 1.98 runs a game, the top ERA in the National League. Among the least of Carlton's accomplishments that season was the shattering of a slew of all-time Philadelphia records.

It was far and away the most spectacular pitching effort of its kind ever achieved in the major leagues. Sandy Koufax had set the modern-day mark for big-league left-handers in 1966, when he also won 27. But Koufax had done it with a Los Angeles Dodgers team that captured 95 games that season. Carlton, getting little back-up support from his teammates, worked his wonders almost single-handedly.

During his singular season, Steve led the National League with a string of achievements: most complete games (30); most starts (41); most innings pitched (346); most wins (27); lowest ERA (1.98); and most strikeouts (310). His strikeout total was probably the most significant. Until that season, the highest number

Carlton finishes his super 1972 season with another win—his 27th.

of strikeouts he had thrown was 210—a full 100 whiffs below his '72 figure.

What was it like to hit against him that year? "It's like trying to drink coffee with a fork," confessed Willie Stargell, the homer-hitting Pittsburgh Pirate.

And how did Steve feel, being the only pitcher ever to win 27 games for a last-place club, and the only pitcher ever to be awarded the Cy Young Award after a season of toiling for a cellar team? "Absolutely great," Carlton said. "Even when the Phillies weren't getting me runs, I refused to recognize pressure. I took every game as it came. When one ended, I started getting ready for the next one. I didn't worry about our team scoring runs. If we scored, great. If we didn't, I just had to pitch hard until we did."

Praise was heaped on Steve. His own pitching coach, Ray Rippelmeyer, said, "I think Steve Carlton is the best pitcher in baseball. I have not seen any pitcher that has three pitches to match his. Fastball, curve and slider. And he gets the ball over the plate. Sometimes you have pitchers with stuff who are wild. But not Steve."

Steve shrugged off the inevitable comparisons made between him and another super-southpaw—Sandy Koufax, the former Dodger ace. "Koufax would have to be the best that ever pitched over a five-year period," he said. "But it's silly to go out chasing a reputation, or to chase somebody's records. Records are something that already happened. All a man can do is go out and pitch each game the best he can. If records fall, they fall."

Nevertheless, Steve began the 1973 season by predicting that he would win 30 games, which would have set a National League record for left-handers. The 28-year-old, with a history of pitching that varied from bad to good to great, declared, "I'm now thinking positive."

"Man is the only one who puts limitations on himself," he explained. "There are really no limits. A lot of professional athletes play beneath their ability . . . because they are not thinking at their peak. The year I lost 19 games, I got all wrapped up in self-pity. I learned a lot about mental attitude that year."

Who could blame Carlton for dreaming the nearly impossible dream? It made sense that, if he could win 27 with a rag-tag team like the Phillies of '72, he just might be able to up the total by three games the next time around. Unfortunately for "Super Steve" and the cause of positive thinking, however, 1973 was not a 30-win season. At no point in '73 did Steve come near repeating his 15 consecutive wins of '72, the 58 straight innings without giving up one earned run, or any of the other remarkable deeds. In fact, he finished the season with a 13–20 record and a 3.93 ERA.

Even his staunchest admirers doubted he would ever repeat the one-in-a-million season he enjoyed that splendid summer of 1972. But that was nothing to cry about. It is given to few men in the sport to be going nowhere one year and then to burst into the record books the next.

Harmon Killebrew

The Killer's Secret Record

Harmon Killebrew, one of the nicest guys ever to wear a baseball uniform, was a killer. He was built like a small tank, 215 solid pounds, with broad shoulders, a thick neck and arms powerful enough to make a blacksmith envious. With one murderous blow, the 5-foot-11 mass of muscles could thunder a baseball 400 feet on a line from home plate to the distant stands.

But Harmon "Killer" Killebrew had one weakness. It was a secret that remained deeply buried in the record books while he enjoyed a career that made pitchers tremble and infielders play *w-a-a-y* back whenever he gripped his menacing bat. To fully appreciate his weakness, though, you must first learn about his strengths.

Speedball pitcher Earl Wilson once thought he knew Harmon's secret. But then in 1970, Wilson said, "A few years ago he definitely had weaknesses. For one thing, he struck out a lot swinging at bad pitches. But now he's a solid hitter who knows the strike zone well. A couple of years ago you could throw a fastball by him, but now I don't think it's wise to challenge him too often. To tell you the truth, if I knew how to pitch to him, I'd do it."

Trying to overpower Killebrew with fastballs got pitchers nowhere but into trouble. Especially in 1969. That was the year the Minnesota Twins' slugger led the major leagues with 49 home runs and 140 runs batted in, drew 145 bases on balls and was voted the American League's Most Valuable Player.

One of his victims that year was Yankee pitcher Jim Bouton. After watching Killebrew slam one of his curve balls out of sight, Bouton felt well-qualified to comment on the emotions felt by the man on the mound as he got set to throw to the Killer. "Mainly fear," was Bouton's reaction. "Two kinds of fear: fear for your life and limbs, should he hit a line drive back at you; and fear of losing your ballgame should he hit one out of the park."

The list of pitchers who suffered at the hands of Harmon Killebrew is a long one. Billy Hoeft has the dubious distinction of being the first to give up a Killebrew clout. And what a clout that was!

The hard-throwing Hoeft was on the mound for the Detroit Tigers. It was a night game, on June 24, 1955, against Killebrew's Senators in Washington's old Griffith Park. (This Washington team later moved to Minnesota and became the Twins, taking Killebrew with them.) The Senators had dropped to seventh place, and the fans were there mostly to boo them. Killebrew, just five days short of his 19th birthday, was anxious to

"The Killer" at bat is an awesome sight.

do something to change those boos to cheers and to lift his team higher in the standings.

"Hoeft is a smart pitcher," Harmon was told by his manager, Cookie Lavagetto. "He throws a fastball that really moves, and he mixes it up with a good curve. Just wait for your pitch and do the best you can."

Killebrew nodded and moved to the plate. The bases were empty as Harmon dug in, settling into his batting stance with the bat cocked high behind his right ear. Hoeft cut loose a fastball that darted past the batter for a called strike. The next two pitches were balls, followed by a slow, curving strike that evened the count at 2–and–2.

The next pitch came in, a blazer about an inch or two below Harmon's shoulders. The baseball had plenty of power behind it, and the young hitter added his own supply of muscle to it. Bat met ball with a resounding *crack.* The crowd, ready to jeer at another strikeout, rose silently to its feet instead. Mouths gaped and eyes widened as the ball rocketed higher and higher, farther and farther. Not until it banged into the 24th row of the bleachers did a sound come from the fans—a roar to match the mighty blast that had bulleted the ball 475 feet. The Killer's first home run had been a monster!

That kind of overwhelming destructiveness, which made Killebrew a terror to pitchers on the field, disappeared as soon as the game ended. Off the field, the soft-spoken infielder was polite and gentle, well-liked by everyone connected with the sport. One of the main things people liked about him was the modesty he maintained as he became more and more successful.

In 1959, for example, Harmon Killebrew was the

most feared batter in an awesome Senator line-up that boasted such sluggers as Jim Lemon, Roy Sievers and Bob Allison. On May 2 of that year, Harmon led the Senators in a 15–3 drubbing of the Detroit Tigers. Killebrew weighed in with a pair of four-baggers in that game, matching his two-homer explosion in the preceding game. Yet, in response to congratulations by teammates and reporters in the locker room, Harmon quietly insisted that he was only one of several long-ball hitters on the club and that the others deserved at least as much credit.

"But you're the really big one," a reporter insisted. "How do you account for your success at hitting those tape-measure jobs? Do you always go for distance?"

Shrugging his bull-like shoulders, Killebrew grinned crookedly and said, "I just go up and try to hit the ball. If they go out, so much the better."

The seasons marched on. With each one the Iowa-born slugger continued to pound out home runs in bunches, earning the reputation of a streak-hitter. He might go for a week without more than a few walks and a few singles, then suddenly erupt with a series of long-range blasts. The word among pitchers was, "When Killebrew's hot, nothing and nobody can cool him down."

Going into the 1959 season, Harmon had a total of 74 home runs. That year he began unloading four-baggers in a style that had everyone talking about "the new Babe Ruth." He hit 42 in 1959, followed by seasons of 31, 46, 48, 45, 49 and a "mere" 25 in 1965, when a serious leg injury sidelined him for a quarter of the schedule.

The Killer came charging back with 39 home runs in 1966, then added 44 more in '67. In 1968 a severely pulled hamstring muscle limited his play to 100 games and his home-run output to 17. Then came his league-leading 49 in 1969, followed by another 41 in '70.

Killebrew suffered more injuries in 1971, and he could contribute only 28 homers to the Twins' cause. On June 22 of that year he clubbed his 498th career round-tripper, then ran into a drought that produced only one more home run over the next month and a half. His injuries, plus the pressure of trying to reach the high hurdle of number 500, had kept his bat from connecting for the big one. Finally, on August 10, he banged out his 500th homer, becoming the tenth major-leaguer to reach that milestone. As he later explained, "Everyone started talking and asking about 500, so I kept trying harder. That's when I felt the pressure."

The pressure was off in 1972, but injuries again limited his HR's to 26 in 139 games. Nevertheless, he had nothing to be ashamed about—not with 541 homers already in his career bag, and more to come. That total moved him into fourth place on the all-time roster of home-run hitters. (Only Babe Ruth, Hank Aaron and Willie Mays had more.) Killebrew could also look back with pride at having won the American League home-run derby in 1962, '63, '64 and '69, and having tied for the 1967 title with Carl Yastrzemski.

So much for the strengths of Harmon Killebrew. Now on to his weakness—and his secret record.

While sluggers like Mays, Aaron and Mantle had the running speed to go along with their powerful hitting,

Killebrew was as slow as a turtle. An inside-the-park home run for the Killer was as likely to occur as an August blizzard in Florida. And *there* is your first real clue to the career-long secret in the baseball life of Harmon Killebrew.

Not only couldn't he fatten his batting average with infield hits, but he was incapable of bunting his way safely to first. The Killer—a mountainous mauler of pitchers—was no more likely to lay down a bunt than he was to swing a bat at a little old lady. In fact, going into the 1973 season, Harmon did not have one sacrifice bunt to his credit. Not one, in 7,254 at-bats, after all his years of outstanding slugging and unselfish play as a major-leaguer.

It's hard to imagine that any batter, slow or fast, would not once be called on to drop a bunt to advance a runner in a tight game. It is even harder to imagine that a team player like Killebrew wouldn't have laid down even one in more than 7,000 at-bats. Yet there it is, standing out boldly in the record book: Fewest Sacrifice Hits—0—Harmon C. Killebrew.

With this in mind, the author decided, in 1973, to ask Harmon about his failure to pick up one sacrifice hit throughout his long and illustrious career. Here's how the conversation went:

Sabin: *Harmon, are you aware that you hold the record for the least number of sacrifice hits in a career—none?*

Killebrew: *No. And, until now, nobody's ever said anything about it, although there have been some comments about my not bunting.*

Sabin: *Do you recall any time that you did have one, and it wasn't recorded?*

The slow-moving Killebrew is out at the plate.

Killebrew: *No. I just haven't been called on to bunt. There have been a lot of situations where I could have tried to move a runner along that way, but managers have never told me to. I've had a lot of sacrifice flies, scoring runners from third, but that's not the same thing as a sacrifice bunt.*

Sabin: *How do you feel about holding such a record?*

Killebrew: *Well, now that we've talked about it, maybe I should go out and bunt one, one of these days. Let's put it this way: I think I could do it if the manager wanted me to. There have been plenty of opportunities, but the managers always told me to hit away, and that's what I did.*

Sabin: *Would you like to break your string of no sacrifice hits?*

Killebrew: *Yes, I think I would. I'll just have to try to lay down a few.*

By the end of 1973, however, Harmon's record was still unsurpassed.

His bat was made for bigger things. And when you can belt a ball out of the park like he could, you don't really have to worry about speed. There's plenty of time to trot around the bases.

Harmon's base-running didn't bother his teammates either, although they often kidded him about it. In one 1973 game against the Baltimore Orioles, the Killer drove in two runs with a long triple that would have been an inside-the-park home run for most other men. (It was only his 24th three-bagger in 14 seasons.) Immediately after Minnesota's 10–3 defeat of the Orioles, Killebrew's teammates nicknamed him "Speedy Gonzalez." Harmon just grinned, enjoying the joke—and the victory.

Then again, perhaps the secret record isn't so strange after all. If a man is a little slow on his way to first and if he has the power to be the fourth greatest home-run hitter in baseball, what kind of manager would make him bunt? After all, Killebrew bunting is a little like hunting mice with a cannon.

Don Drysdale

A String of Zeroes

"I may be in a groove where I'm throwing a little harder and a little sharper right now, but I think I'm pitching about as well as last year. You can pitch just as well and maybe give up a run or two. You need luck for a shutout. I had no luck last year. That's baseball."

These were the words of Don Drysdale in 1968. The big, hard-throwing, right-hander could have added that you need runs, as well as luck, to win. That year his Los Angeles Dodger teammates gave so little hitting support that Drysdale was the only starting pitcher on the staff to finish the season with a winning record (14–12). But when he made that statement about luck, Don was in the middle of a record-shattering pitching streak that would have won games even with a line-up of Little Leaguers.

Glory and winning big games were nothing new to

Don Drysdale. The fiercely competitive pitcher had won the Cy Young Award in 1962, his 25–9 won–lost record earning him the distinction as baseball's best pitcher that year. In 1965 he posted a 23–12 record. There had been a couple of bad years, too (1966 and '67), when he won 13 and lost 16 each season. But bad or good, no season could compare to this one in the career of Don Drysdale.

The streak began on May 14, with Big Don outdueling Ferguson Jenkins to defeat the Chicago Cubs, 1–0. Four days later, the 6-foot-6, 220-pound hurler led the Dodgers to another 1–0 victory, beating the Houston Astros and pitcher Dave Giusti. Four more days and Drysdale registered another whitewash job, topping the St. Louis Cardinals and their great pitching star, Bob Gibson. In that game Don's teammates managed to collect a pair of runs, for a 2–0 win and Don's third shutout in a row.

Shutout number four came on May 26. Again Big D blanked the Astros, but this time the Dodgers hardly needed it, scoring five runs to win 5–0. Drysdale yielded just six hits to Houston. In the ninth inning, he gave up two of the six hits. He also hit one batter and walked another. But Dodger second baseman Paul Popovich saved the shutout by starting a double play, and Drysdale wrapped it up himself by getting the last Houston batter to ground out with the bases loaded. After the game Drysdale—soaked in sweat and clearly exhausted—told reporters, "I don't think I could have thrown even one more pitch."

Luckily, he didn't have to throw another pitch in a ballgame for the next four days. Although Don nor-

The Dodgers' hard-throwing Don Drysdale goes into his windup.

mally started every fourth day, Dodger manager Walter Alston decided to let him have an extra day of rest before starting the first game of a home stand against the league-leading San Francisco Giants.

Drysdale's mound opponent on the night of May 31 would be Mike McCormick, the 1967 Cy Young Award winner. But the Giant who spelled special trouble was Willie Mays. Before the game Willie was told that Drysdale would be out to try to tie the major-league record of five consecutive shutouts. The mark, set by Guy "Doc" White of the Chicago White Sox, had been in the book since 1904.

"How do you think you'll do against Drysdale tonight?" Mays was asked. "Alston says that Don's throwing faster than he has in years."

Although Mays responded with a grin, his words were serious: "He doesn't throw as hard as he once did, but he can throw everything right where he wants it now. I'll just do my best, like I do against any pitcher."

When Drysdale was asked how he felt about having to face hitters like Mays and Willie McCovey in such an important game, he said, "I feel as good as ever; but I have to admit this streak does have me keyed up and more nervous than usual."

That night Drysdale finished his warm-up to the rhythmic clapping of 45,000 fans, a sound that would continue throughout the game. The first batter he faced was the pesky Ron Hunt, who would do anything to get on base. Big Don led off with a fastball to the outside corner, and Hunt lofted an easy fly for out number one.

Jim Davenport, the second batter, jumped on a curve and rifled a clean single to left. Then Willie Mays marched up to take his swings. Several pitches later Willie was marching back to the dugout, Don's first strikeout victim. Mays' place at the plate was taken by Willie McCovey. Always a dangerous slugger, McCovey had an especially good record against Drysdale. ("McCovey," Don once said, "would get out of a hospital bed to face me.") But the pitcher kept the ball in tight, getting two strikes on McCovey before throwing him a sinker. McCovey slapped an easy grounder for the inning-ending out.

Zero after zero appeared on the scoreboard, and the fans inched forward on their seats. In each of the first six innings, Giants reached base only to have Don's strong right arm and some equally strong Dodger fielding prevent them from scoring. Along with their glove-work, Don's teammates also helped ease the pressure by giving him two runs early in the game.

Drysdale seemed to grow more confident as the game went on. In the seventh and eighth innings he retired the Giants in order. Then in the ninth inning he gave up his first walk of the game to leadoff batter Willie Mc-Covey. Jim Ray Hart followed with a line single, which moved McCovey to second. Five pitches later Drysdale had walked his second batter, Dave Marshall, filling the bases with none out.

Dodger catcher Jeff Torborg walked out to the mound. He wanted to relax Drysdale, who was clearly weary and showing the strain of reaching for a record. Torborg looked at Walter Alston for a sign that he wanted to bring in a relief pitcher. Even though it was a risky decision, with Los Angeles' 3–0 lead in jeopardy, the Dodger manager indicated he would stick with his pitcher. As Alston said after the game, "There was no way I'd lift Don until he gave up that first run."

Giant catcher Dick Dietz stepped into the batter's box, and Torborg settled into his crouch. Four pitches later, with the count 2–and–2, Drysdale angled a slider toward the inside corner. It was breaking too far inside but, instead of jumping out of the way, Dietz just lifted his left arm to protect his face. The ball struck his elbow. Dietz dropped his bat and started trotting to first as the three base runners began to move up.

"Come back," umpire Harry Wendelstedt called to Dietz. Wendelstedt said that Dietz could not take first because he had not made an effort to avoid being hit by the pitch.

The Giants argued angrily, but the dispute ended with the umpire's decision standing and Giant manager Herman Franks being thrown out of the game. Play resumed with a 3-and–2 count. Dietz fouled off the next two pitches, then lifted a fly to left fielder Jim Fairey. Fairey caught it and rifled the ball home, holding the runners where they were. The next batter, Ty Cline, bounced a low fastball to first baseman Wes Parker, who threw home in time to force the runner dashing in from third. Parker made the next play, too, gloving an easy pop-up off the bat of pinch-hitter Jack Hiatt to end the game. Final score: 3–0.

Big Don had tied the 64-year-old record with his fifth shutout in a row. But he still had a long way to go before he could even think of relaxing. The next day's sport pages announced that Don needed just one more shutout to have the record all to himself. Of course he knew that. But something he hadn't known was also revealed there: the 45 consecutive scoreless innings he had put together had moved him close to Carl Hubbell's 35-year-old National League mark of 46⅓ consecutive scoreless innings and within reach of Walter Johnson's 55-year-old major-league record of 56 innings of uninterrupted non-run pitching.

Tuesday night, June 4, 1968, was cold and cloudy as Big D prepared to take on the Pittsburgh Pirates. It was a tough batting order, featuring long-ball hitters Roberto Clemente and Willie Stargell and such crafty batsmen as Manny Mota, Maury Wills and Bill Mazeroski. Holding them scoreless would be a challenge under normal circumstances, but it was twice as rough with a record riding on every pitch. One mistake to someone like Clemente or Stargell would see Don's shutout string broken by a long drive into the stands. Or a walk to Maury Wills might have the shrewd base stealer off and running on the next pitch, working his way around to third, coming home on a hit or sacrifice fly.

With 30,000 Dodger Stadium fans rooting for the "local boy" born in nearby Van Nuys, Drysdale got set to take on a team that had knocked him out of the box the last 14 times he had faced them. Pittsburgh's leadoff man was Matty Alou, who tried to bunt his way on. Alou was thrown out at first—as was Maury Wills, who tried the same strategy. Drysdale retired the third Pirate batter to chalk up his first zero of the night. With that zero, Drysdale registered his 46th straight scoreless inning.

Then the Dodgers came to bat against Pirate ace Jim Bunning. Continuing the weak hitting that made the '68

Don fires a fastball past Bill Mazeroski to set a National League record of
46 2/3 consecutive scoreless innings.

Dodgers known as a "good pitch, no hit" team, Los Angeles failed to score. Big Don strode out to start the second inning, aware that he had to get just one more out to tie Hubbell's mark. Roberto Clemente was the batter, and he pounded a low serve past the pitcher's mound. The ball was headed for center field, but Paul Popovich scooted over, gloved it and threw to Wes Parker for the big out.

Up next, Manny Mota was hit by a high, inside pitch. The ball struck his batting helmet and, uninjured, he took first. As he inched off the bag, veteran infielder Bill Mazeroski almost destroyed Drysdale's dream by sending a screaming drive down the left-field line. But the ball curved foul, and Maz went down swinging on the next pitch. With that out, Drysdale's name replaced Hubbell's in the record book.

Now Don's sights were set on Walter Johnson's mark of 56 straight scoreless innings. The Dodgers reached Bunning for five runs, while Drysdale maintained his mastery over the Pirate bats. He yielded a double to pinch-hitter Gary Kolb in the fifth inning and a single to Maury Wills in the ninth. But nobody in a Pirate uniform scored. And with Willie Stargell's second-to-first ground-out ending the game, Drysdale had captured his sixth consecutive shutout—and another major-league record.

"Great pitching, Don," a sportswriter said to him in the dressing room. "Now you go after Johnson's mark. But how do these records make you feel?"

"It's a great thrill," Drysdale said, accepting congratulations from the teammates and sportswriters crowding around him. "I just had to get it over with one way or another. I couldn't have stood the strain much longer. I've never felt pressure like that." He paused. "As for Johnson . . . Well, we'll see how it goes against the Phillies."

The Philadelphia Phillies weren't known for their big bats, but they were hoping to spoil Don's run for the record anyway. They couldn't do it in the first inning, as Cookie Rojas flied out, John Briggs walked, Tony Gonzalez hit a ground ball that was used to force Briggs out at second, and Johnny Callison flied out. Now Drysdale's streak had reached 55 innings.

Needing three more outs to match Johnson's mark, Don opened the second inning by getting Bill White and Tony Taylor to hit the ball to the infield for two easy plays. Then he carried the count to 3–and–2 on Clay Dalrymple, leaned back and fired a blazer past the Phillie catcher for the strikeout—the out that meant 56 consecutive no-run innings!

The top of the third brought Roberto Pena to the plate. His face grimly set, Drysdale mixed curves with fastballs, inside and outside. A fastball—strike one. A sharp-breaking curve—strike two. Another curve—fouled away. A fastball, outside—ball one. Another fastball—fouled past third. Then Pena got enough wood on the next pitch to top a slow roller down the third-base line. Ken Boyer sprinted in, grabbed the ball and threw it to first, beating Pena by a split second. With that big out, Drysdale had passed the great Walter Johnson!

Don kept his streak going through the fourth inning, but in the fifth singles by Tony Taylor and Clay Dalrymple put Philly runners at first and third.

Drysdale is congratulated by Sandy Koufax, another Dodger great, after Don's shutout streak of 58 2/3 innings was finally broken.

Drysdale bore down and blew a third strike by Pena, only to have Howie Bedell score Taylor with a sacrifice fly to left-center field. The final score was Dodgers, 5–Phillies, 3.

It was all over. During 25 nerve-tingling days of rising tension and falling records, Don Drysdale pitched six consecutive shutouts and 58⅔ straight scoreless innings. His string of zeroes had added up to two major-league records.

Al Kaline and Ted Williams

Two Sides of the Coin

The scouting report on the high school ballplayer read: "It is very doubtful he will hit major-league pitching well enough to make the grade as an outfielder. I recommend that we look at him as a shortstop or a second baseman, as he has excellent tools for an infielder."

The man who wrote that report was John McHale, farm director of the Detroit Tigers in 1953. The player referred to was Al Kaline, who was then an 18-year-old graduate of Southern High School in Baltimore, Maryland. Two years later, McHale was sitting in Detroit's Briggs Stadium, watching Tiger right fielder Al Kaline show him how wrong he had been. And McHale was delighted.

The Tigers were playing the Kansas City Athletics. In the first inning Kaline walked. In the third he lifted a home run over the left-field screen off pitcher Johnny Gray. In the fourth he drilled a single off Charley Bishop. Kaline was seeing the ball "real well," and in the sixth inning he really put his bat to work. He picked out a Bob Spicer fastball and hammered it almost 400 feet into the left-center-field stands. The Tigers batted around, bringing the right-handed Kaline to the plate for the second time in that inning. Spicer had been replaced by Bob Trice, but that made no difference to Al. The "doubtful" hitting prospect removed any remaining shreds of doubt about his ability by driving one of Trice's serves out of the park for his second homer of the inning.

That second four-bagger marked the first time in history that a Detroit player ever hit two home runs in one inning. It was also the first time any American Leaguer had done it since Joe DiMaggio turned the trick in 1936. In all, Al's contribution to the Tigers' 16–0 rout of the Athletics was four hits in five at-bats, three runs scored and six RBI's.

That outburst took place on April 17, 1955. It was a good indication of what the American League could expect from the 6-foot-1, 175-pound Kaline for the rest of the season. He impressed everyone with his fielding, running and throwing. But most impressive was the way he continued to hit, and hit hard, winding up with 27 home runs, 8 triples and 24 doubles.

The blond-haired kid who had jumped from the sandlots to the big leagues closed out his second full season with a .340 batting average. That was really news. He was exactly 20 years and 280 days old the day he was declared the batting champion of the American

League. It made Albert William Kaline the youngest batting king of all time. By gaining that honor he replaced another Detroit hitter by the name of Ty Cobb, who had won the title with a .350 average back in 1907 when he was a few days older than Kaline.

In the years that followed 1955, Kaline continued to stroke the ball at a steady .300 clip, but he never again won a batting crown. Asked why, in 1968, he blamed his early success. "It was the worst thing that ever happened to me," he explained. "Sure, it was great winning the title, but it put a lot of pressure on me the following seasons, when I didn't reach that .340 mark again. People expected me to go from .340 on up. It was a handicap and a hard thing to adjust to."

A number of people tried to help Al duplicate his greatest season. Among them was a fanatic student of the art of hitting, Ted Williams. Even though Williams wanted to win every batting crown himself, he was not the least bit selfish about offering advice, even to a player who might stand between him and those titles.

"From the first day I met Ted," Kaline said, "he freely gave me tips on how to improve myself. He impressed me with the importance of having strong wrists to make a quicker swing possible, and strong arms and shoulders for power."

Kaline took Williams' advice, and was forever grateful to Ted for all the help he gave.

Theodore Samuel Williams batted .356 in Al's title-winning year, 16 points higher than Kaline. But Ted didn't have enough official at-bats to qualify for the batting championship. If he had, Williams would have wound up as the AL hitting leader seven times—instead of the six he had to "settle for."

Williams was the most dedicated hitter ever to wear spikes. Even after he had retired with a lifetime batting average of .344, the left-handed slugger would still talk about putting a bat to a ball with the total enthusiasm of a rookie. "When I played," he said, "I had a goal. I wanted people to remember me as the greatest hitter that ever lived." And many believe he was.

Williams also said, "Now I look around and there's no question in my mind that hitters are not as good as they were. The game is not getting the caliber of athlete it used to. Kids today don't have dedication. Their parents have all this extra leisure time so the kids go on vacation. Or if they stay home they watch television. When I was growing up, between the ages of nine and 17, *all I did* was learn hitting. From morning until night. And I lived in San Diego, so that was all year round. That's the kind of dedication it takes to be a hitter."

Williams with a bat in his hands was the picture of a man who had come to hit. An earthquake wouldn't have broken his concentration. At 6-foot-4 and 200 pounds, he looked like a potential murderer as he glared out at the pitcher. He'd grind the bat in his hands, as if to dig grooves into the handle for a firmer grip. Then he'd take his wide-open stance, plant his feet exactly where he wanted them and not move a fraction of an inch from that position. His eyes, his hands, every muscle in his body—everything about Ted Williams seemed to be warning the pitcher, "I'm here to hit."

For 19 seasons he buggy-whipped his bat around in one of the most breathtakingly beautiful, explosively

Al Kaline, the youngest batting champ ever, got a few pointers . . .

. . . from super-slugging Ted Williams, the oldest.

powerful swings ever seen on a baseball field. For 19 seasons he brought glory to himself and the Boston Red Sox, hammering out 521 home runs among the 2,654 hits that went to make up one of the highest lifetime averages ever recorded. He set a major-league mark by receiving at least one intentional walk in each of 19 consecutive games. He tied Babe Ruth's major-league records for leading both leagues in bases on balls four times; and for most consecutive seasons (also four) leading the league in bases on balls.

There was a good reason for all those walks, as many pitchers well knew. A walk to Williams meant no worry that he would rocket a ball against the right-field wall—or over it. Giving Williams a base on balls was one way to prevent him from taking four. Ted gave pitchers the sweats for 19 seasons, but it would have been 25 if he hadn't been sidelined by injury one year and spent five of his potentially most productive years in military service. For example, Ted was the last man to bat over .400, in 1941, by hitting .406. Who knows what he might have done if he hadn't been in the service from 1943 through 1945? And the same thoughts apply when consideration is given to his home-run totals.

It was no surprise when Ted was named the American League's Most Valuable Player in 1946 and 1949. The only surprise was that he didn't win the award more times than that.

Williams' career was a series of remarkable accomplishments. Yet there were two that, for a very special reason, were absolutely phenomenal. One was that, in winning his fifth batting title, in 1957, he became the oldest batting champion of all time.

Soon after that season, Kansas City pitcher Ned Garver recalled, "The word around the league was that Ted was slipping a little . . . starting to check his swing. He never did this before. Well, the next time I pitched against him, I was looking for him to ease up on the swing. I threw him a high knuckle ball, and he hit it into the bleachers. That was the last time I listened to that kind of talk."

Including that homer off Garver, The Splendid Splinter, as the tall, slender slugger was called, banged out enough hits to average a fantastic .388 for the 1957 season. A batting king at the ripe old age of 39!

To top it all off, Ted came back the next year with still another incredible feat. A middle-aged, 40-year-old baseball player was rare enough. But for one to hit .328, as Ted did in 1958, was truly to dip into the Fountain of Youth. By winning his sixth batting crown, Williams broke his own record as the oldest batting champ in the history of the sport.

Al Kaline was 20 years old when he won his first batting crown—Williams was twice that age when he won his last. There are new slugging champs every year, but there may never be one as young as Kaline or as old as the great Ted Williams.

Sam McDowell

The Ups and Downs of Sudden Sam

Major-leaguers have a variety of colorful words to describe a truly *fast* fastball. "Smoke" is one; "blazer," "swift" and "burner" are others. Sandy Koufax threw smoke, as did a couple of Bobs named Gibson and Feller. And, of course, the king of all speedballers was Walter Johnson. All of them are Hall-of-Famers, except Gibson, whose election is just a matter of time.

And then there's Sam McDowell. He was nicknamed Sudden Sam after one of his strikeout victims described a McDowell fastball with these awe-filled words: "It reaches you all of a sudden."

Sudden Sam threw smoke, as blindingly fast as anyone. But when the day comes to nominate him for a plaque in the Hall of Fame, there will be many an argument among the voters. "Look at his strikeout record," one will say in Sam's defense. And an anti-

Sudden Sam gets set to throw a burner in his early days with the Indians.

McDowell voice will snap back, "Oh yeah? Look at his bases-on-balls record." Then they'll start digging into the miserable and marvelous sides of the roller-coaster career of Sam McDowell.

Toeing the rubber, Sudden Sam was a fearsome sight to the bravest of batters. As they got set to hit they would see a face fixed in grim lines, heavy-browed eyes slitted in concentration and a huge left hand wrapped around a baseball that seemed to have shrunk in size. That was the physical threat the 6-foot-6, 215-pound giant posed. Then there was the chilling fact that his control was far from perfect. In fact, a Sudden Sam special had as much chance of booming toward the batter's head as toward the catcher's mitt.

It's not that Sam tried to intimidate anyone—he just couldn't help it! "If it takes deliberate throwing at batters to win 30, forget it," he said. "Beanballs and knockdowns are cheating. Because when you cheat you aren't winning. You are defeating yourself in a way. I'm even afraid to throw brushback pitches, which are not knockdowns. They scare me, too, because I could kill somebody even though I'm only trying to keep them from digging in on me."

Nevertheless, big-league hitters never dug in very deep on Sudden Sam. Scared or simply overpowered by the McDowell fastball, batters had great respect for Sam's arm. So did his own teammates. After a game relief pitcher Dick Radatz once told McDowell that he had thrown four no-hitters in high school.

"I pitched 21," said Sam.

"Twenty-one no-hit games?" Radatz repeated slowly. "*Twenty-one* no-hit games?"

"Counting Little League and Colt League and all," Sam said, "it was 40. Then with two in the minors, that makes 42."

Radatz considered this information for a moment, then said, "Man, you don't deserve no more."

From the day he joined the Cleveland Indians in 1964, the 21-year-old rookie from Monroeville, Pennsylvania, began a pitching pattern of ups and downs that would become his trademark. That year he posted an 11–6 won-lost record, struck out 177 men and walked 100. But his fine earned run average of 2.71 was offset by all the walks he surrendered, not to mention the 148 hits he allowed in 173 innings.

"Cut down on those walks," he was told, "and you've got it made." Sam certainly tried, but in 1965 he threw ball four to 132 batters and yielded 178 hits. The 325 strikeouts he chalked up, however, helped balance the books. That strikeout total was just 23 short of the all-time American League high set in 1946 by another great Cleveland speedballer, Robert Feller.

To fully appreciate that achievement you need to know that Sam pitched 98 fewer innings than Rapid Robert did in 1946. Since McDowell averaged well above a strikeout an inning, it's obvious that he would have far surpassed Feller's record had he appeared in an equal number of innings.

Asked to compare his ability to fan batters with Feller's, McDowell said, "I don't really know *how* to strike a guy out. If Tebbetts [the Cleveland manager] came and told me, 'Sam, strike out the next batter,' I wouldn't know where to begin. The minute I *try* to strike out a batter, the minute I start to think about it,

I'm dead. The guy gets a hit. Actually, batters strike themselves out."

Day after day throughout that starry 1965 season, Sam was interviewed for newspapers, magazines and television. He finished his sophomore season with a 17–11 won–lost record. But the best part of the story was his league-leading 2.18 earned run average. That ERA tied the all-time Indian record, another Feller milestone. A corner of the Hall of Fame was reserved, in the minds of many, to hold baseballs and other mementos associated with "the new Feller," or "the new Koufax."

Then came 1966—a very different chapter in the Sam McDowell story. His strikeout total, although it topped the AL for the second straight year, dipped to 225. At the same time, his ERA rose to 2.88. This year he gave up 102 walks and 130 hits. And worst of all, he won only nine games while losing eight.

"An off-year," some apologists said. "Arm troubles affected his pitching," said others. "Just wait—he'll be a real winner next year."

Next year, 1967, saw another good strikeout campaign by Sudden Sam. He nailed opposing batters with 236 strikeouts—but they also reached him for 201 hits and 123 walks. His 13 wins against 15 losses couldn't be defended, even by his most devoted fans, nor could his 3.85 ERA.

Sam was still as sudden as ever, but suddenly he was no longer being ranked with the great pitchers. As one columnist told his readers: "Watching McDowell pitch is like seeing a man pour diamonds down a drain. What a waste of talent. An arm like that should make the man rich and famous, but he refuses to listen to his manager, his pitching coach and his catchers. They can see what he's doing wrong, but he insists he knows best. They all want to help him and he won't let them."

Someone may have gotten through to Sam before opening day of 1968, because that year he recaptured enough of his form to storm back with 283 strikeouts and an acceptable 15–13 won–lost mark. However, the 180 hits and 110 walks he gave up made his fans and critics wonder if he would ever settle down. This was the memorable Year of the Pitcher, and the American League's mound star was Denny McLain, who won 31 and lost 6. Sam McDowell's name was nowhere near the top of the list when it came to grading pitchers in both leagues.

The clouds over Sudden's head cleared a bit in 1969. His 2.94 ERA wasn't brilliant, but it was the tenth best in the AL. His 18–14 won–lost record wasn't great, either, but it wasn't bad. The 102 walks he issued and the 222 hits he gave up could almost be overlooked in light of his 279 strikeouts—the most in either league.

Sam's confidence, never really in danger no matter what his records showed, really bloomed in 1970. So what if he led the majors with 131 bases on balls? He also outdid all AL and NL hurlers in the strikeout department, with 304. And while he threw 17 wild pitches and was pounded for 236 hits, that didn't bother him a bit when he closed out the year as a 20-game winner.

All through that winter he was getting set to tear into the American League. "I am going to win 30 games in 1971," he told anyone who would listen. And just to make sure that every baseball fan in America got the message, he wrote an article called "How I'll Win 30 This Year" for a national magazine. "Last year I shot only for victories," he informed his readers. "And still I got 300 K's. Most of them came on my breaking pitches, not my fastball. Watch me surprise a lot of hitters this summer by pitching them into ground balls, not strikeouts. I've developed a sinker-ball which is now perfect. Let 'em hit it into the ground; I've got a team behind me. And I have a couple of other surprises for the hitters . . . I like to come up with something new every year, either a different pitch or a new wrinkle in my delivery. You never know what I'll suddenly come up with. That's why they call me Sudden."

Unfortunately, that *wasn't* why they called him Sudden, and that wasn't the way things turned out at all. He did surprise the hitters—and lots of other people—by refusing to pitch early in the season because of a contract dispute. Still, Sam showed up enough times to win 13 and lose 17. That totalled 30 all right, but not the 30 wins he had promised. He also finished with a 3.39 ERA, not a figure to boost the confidence of a major-league management having serious doubts about a very well-paid pitcher. Cleveland proved its loss of confidence by trading Sam to the San Francisco Giants before the start of the next season.

The 1972 season had to be the most miserable one of Sam's baseball life. He was battered for an average of 4.34 runs a game, and only some timely power-hitting by his new Giant teammates enabled him to win more games than he lost. Along with his 10–8 record, he struck out 122 and walked 86.

Then came 1973 and the most crushing blow of all to the pride of Sam McDowell. The Giants dropped him from their starting line-up and sent him out to the bull pen. Now the once-golden arm was used only in relief.

Sam struggled along that way for several weeks, then awoke one morning to find himself back in the American League. The Yankees thought enough of Sam to want him on their staff as a starter, and they paid the Giants over $100,000 to get him.

The New Yorkers were gunning for a pennant, and they thought Sam McDowell might just be able to help them. In his first appearances he made the Yankees look wise by picking up a pair of quick wins. But then, in a mid-season contest against the Boston Red Sox, his old control woes came back with a rush. In one inning he served up three walks and a double. In six innings he walked a total of seven men. Yet, somehow, the Sox managed to score just one run, and relief help from Sparky Lyle saved the victory.

After the game a reporter reminded Sam that he had walked three batters on twelve straight pitches in the fourth inning, only to be saved by getting the next batter to fly out to end the threat. Then, in the next two innings, he had walked the first man up. "How does it happen, Sam?" the writer asked.

"You lose confidence in yourself," a subdued McDowell explained. "Then you start aiming the ball and lose 50 percent of your effectiveness. I've been through it before and I don't enjoy it, but it doesn't worry me, either," he added, confident once more.

"The trouble is," Sam went on, "that I haven't

Pitching for the Yankees in 1973, Sam had more downs than ups.

thrown my best pitches yet this year. As a relief pitcher you just try to blow it by them. Now that I'm a starter again, I'm just getting things together."

After eight years as a big-league pitcher, Sudden Sam was still trying to get things together. It was another way of saying that he had lost his way on the road to glory. Oh, there *was* some glory. While walking that road, he threw his fastballs and other assorted pitches past enough batters to reach twelfth place on the all-time career strikeout list. In addition, he set the record of most strikeouts in three consecutive games, with 40 in 1968, a mark that eluded the best smoke-throwers in both leagues. But along that same road he dealt out walks galore, setting a pair of records no self-respecting pitcher would ever want to come near. Sudden Sam was the number one major-league pitcher to lead both leagues in total walks over a season. By committing that crime five different years, he also established the modern-era mark of most seasons leading the American League in bases on balls.

His career hadn't developed quite the way the unpredictable southpaw expected, but he certainly made the record books. For his best and his worst, nobody is likely to forget Sam McDowell.

Mickey Mantle

Homers and Strikeouts

There is a baseball in the Cooperstown Hall of Fame. It was catapulted out of Washington's Griffith Stadium on April 17, 1953, by a young Yankee named Mickey Charles Mantle, then in his third major league season. What was so special about this baseball—just one of hundreds Mantle would smash out of ballparks in the course of a homer-packed career that lasted almost 20 years? To find out, let's go back to that day and see it happen.

The Washington Senator pitcher Chuck Stobbs was preparing to throw to Mantle, who was batting left-handed. Mickey was sometimes called The Sweet Switcher because he could bang a baseball out of shape swinging from either side of the plate. The New York center fielder was feeling especially strong that day, which was saying a lot: even on an average day the

6-foot, 200-pounder was a menace to American League pitchers.

Stobbs delivered a fastball that approached the plate at the level of the letters on Mickey's uniform. Mantle uncoiled furiously. The heavy part of his bat met the ball with the sound of an exploding hand grenade. Thousands of fans turned their heads in unison to follow the ball as it climbed higher and higher.

By the time Mantle churned past first, the ball had already cleared the fence in left-center field. The distance from home plate to that point was 391 feet. Seventy feet beyond the fence was a wall 60 feet high. The speeding ball flew over that, too, but struck a sign on top of the wall—460 feet from the catcher—and bounced somewhere out of sight.

When the ball was finally recovered, it was determined that if the ball had not been obstructed it would have landed a full 565 feet from the plate. In all of baseball history, that was the longest official home run ever recorded.

Home runs—tape-measure jobs and the more ordinary sort—were a specialty of the Yankee slugger who spearheaded his team to twelve pennants in 14 seasons. Batting from both sides of the plate, Mickey slammed 535 four-baggers in 18 years of regular-season play. While that figure didn't come close to the career totals amassed by Babe Ruth and Henry Aaron, Mantle had enough records of his own. The blond-haired bomber from Commerce, Oklahoma, winner of baseball's Triple Crown (home runs, batting average and runs batted in) in 1956 and three-time recipient of the American League's Most Valuable Player Award, put together a

After hitting his fantastic 565-foot homer, Mickey Mantle is congratulated by Yogi Berra.

chain of career records that elevated him to the rare Olympian heights shared by the Babe and Hammerin' Hank.

Mantle was the greatest slugger in World Series history—and since his team played in the Series twelve times, he had plenty of chances to prove it. In his 63 Series games—a WS record itself—he racked up 18 round-trippers to break Babe Ruth's record of 15.

And when the subject was driving in World Series runs, Mantle's name had to be the first one spoken. In his twelve world-championship clashes between 1951 and 1964, Mickey collected 40 RBI's. But that wasn't all. He also headed the list for most runs scored (42), most extra-base hits (26), most total bases (123) and most bases on balls (43).

Mantle was human, though, and among his record-breaking achievements are a couple he would have been delighted not to own. First, during the same 63 World Series contests, the super-slugger was a strikeout victim 54 times! And his career strikeout record is one of the truly amazing figures in the book. In 18 seasons, he struck out 1,710 times, a mark that may never be equalled.

To be fair to Mantle, it should be shown that he also had more than 2,400 hits and that he walked even more often than he struck out (1,734 bases on balls). But the fact remains: no one in baseball's history ever went down swinging as many times as the Yankees' Mickey Mantle.

Another more recent strikeout record is even more amazing. Where Mantle averaged fewer than 100 strikeouts per season and never whiffed more than 126 times,

Mantle takes a mighty swing—and strikes out.

Bobby Bonds of the San Francisco Giants struck out 189 times in 1970! Why did the Giants keep such an inept swinger, you may ask. The answer is simple: in the same season, Bonds had more than 200 hits, batted for a .302 average and stole 48 bases.

The lesson for future strikeout kings is clear. If you are hitting .300 or leading the league in home runs, no one will complain if you set a strikeout record along the way. But if you are hitting .220 and your hits never leave the infield, your strikeout totals will probably break only one unhappy record: fastest trip back to the minor leagues.

Bob Gibson

The Pitcher Who Never Gave Up

The word "quit" just wasn't in the vocabulary of pitcher Bob Gibson. A strong right arm brought him to the top of the list of super-pitchers; but an even stronger will to win kept him there. Overcoming sickness, pitching with pain, staying on the mound inning after inning as the last drop of energy drained from his body—the Cardinal ace never gave up.

Because he suffered from arthritis in his pitching elbow, the 6-foot-1, 195-pound flame-thrower needed at least four days off between starting assignments. Under ordinary circumstances, he got that rest. But circumstances were far from ordinary during the 1964 World Series when the St. Louis Cardinals met the New York Yankees. Gibson lost the first game he threw against the power-packed Yanks, 8–3. But he came back to win the fifth game of the Series, 5–2. And after just two days of

Bob Gibson seems to sail off the mound after releasing a pitch.

rest he was on the mound again, facing the Bronx Bombers in the final meeting to decide the championship.

For the first three and a half innings neither side scored. Then the Cards exploded with three runs in the fourth and three more in the fifth. Gibson was on top 6–0 going into the sixth, but the game was far from over. By then everyone could see that the St. Louis fireballer was running out of steam. As he toed the rubber, the scorching sun beat down on Busch Stadium, pushing the temperature over the 100-degree mark. Sweat streamed down Gibson's face, his chest heaved with each breath he took, and only he knew how extreme was the pain in his right elbow.

At this point the courageous right-hander was throwing as much with his heart as with his arm. The Yankees began to fight back. Bobby Richardson opened the New York half of the sixth with a single, and Roger Maris followed with another. Then Mickey Mantle came up to bat. The muscular slugger weighed into the first pitch, hammering it out of the park and bringing the two base runners home. Suddenly the Cardinal lead was sliced in half, and manager Johnny Keane walked out to talk with Gibson.

"How do you feel?" Keane asked, fully aware that his pitcher was dead tired.

"I feel fine," Gibson answered, with no hesitation at all.

Keane slapped Bob on the back and, after telling him "I want you to finish this," returned to the dugout.

And finish it he did, conquering fatigue, pain, and hit-hungry Yankees for three more innings, to clinch the title contest 7–5. He also clinched a new seven-game Series record for himself, striking out a total of 31 men in the three games he pitched.

Why had Keane kept Gibson in after the Yankees had bombarded him with three runs? "I was committed to Bob's heart," Keane said simply. "Bob is a real thoroughbred."

And what was Gibson feeling when Keane came out to the mound? As the Cardinal pitcher explained in his autobiography, *From Ghetto to Glory*: "I wouldn't have cared if I was keeling over out there, I would never say I was tired. You never feel you're not the right guy to do the job unless you're hurt. It goes with having confidence in yourself. You could be out on your feet and they could be beating your brains out, and you still think you're the best and you can get them out. This is the feeling you have to have. Very few guys give up, and that's what you'd be doing if you told the manager you were tired. You would be giving up."

Throughout his long career, the idea of giving up never once entered Gibson's mind. In fact, it was when things got really tough that he bore down the hardest, reaching deep inside for the extra courage and skill that said: Here's a real pro.

Robert Gibson first joined the Cardinals near the end of the 1959 season. There he was, a man whose childhood had been filled with weakness and sickness. Pneumonia, which had almost taken his life once, returned to plague him time and time again. Gibson also suffered from asthma, which affected his breathing, and from hay fever, a rheumatic heart and rickets, which weakened his bones. All in all he hardly seemed a good prospect for the majors. And although his pitching showed great promise, he won only six of the first 17 games he pitched in 1959 and '60. But Gibson hadn't come that far only to give up!

In 1961, Bob's early promise became a reality when he won 13 and lost 12 for St. Louis. Then Bob really hit his stride. From 1962 through 1966 he won 93 games. In that same five-season stretch he struck out 1,152 batters.

The 1967 campaign should have been Bob's third consecutive 20-win season. But in July of that year a line drive struck—and broke—his right leg. By early September, the cast was off the leg, and the gutty pitcher was back on the mound. Gibson finished the season with a 13–7 record, but his work wasn't over yet. The Cards had captured the National League pennant, and Bob was their number one weapon in the World Series against the Boston Red Sox.

There he was, almost 32 years old, coming off a season in which he had been badly injured. But the man who wouldn't quit simply knuckled down to his job. He beat the Red Sox, 2–1, in the opening game, giving up six hits and striking out ten. In the fourth game he blanked the Sox, 6–0, giving up five hits and striking out six. His third and last appearance came in the seventh and deciding game. When he walked off the mound nine innings later, the Cardinals were champions and Bob had his third victory of the Series, a 7–2 win.

Injury, weakness, weariness—nothing had prevented Gibson from proving he was the best. With that victory Bob Gibson had tied five World Series records: Most Complete Games Won, Consecutive, Total Series, 5 (three in 1967 and the two he had gotten in 1964, his last

Gibson writhes in pain after his leg was broken by Roberto Clemente's hard line drive in a 1967 game.

Series appearance); Most Games Won in One Series, 3; Most Consecutive Games Won in One Series, 3; Most Games Won, Losing None, in One Series, 3; Most Complete Games in One Series, 3.

Impressive, yes. But all that was completely over-shadowed by Bob's 1968 heroics. The competition he faced that year was as tough as it could be. It came not only from batters but from other pitchers as well. Major-league pitching was so phenomenal in '68 that it will always be referred to as the Year of the Pitcher. The awesome list of 20-game winners that season included such stars as Juan Marichal, Don Drysdale, Ferguson Jenkins, Denny McLain and Dave McNally. But great as they all were, to most American fans Bob Gibson was *the* pitcher of 1968.

Gibson was unquestionably the National League's king of the hill. His 22–9 won–lost mark, the best of his career, carried the Cardinals to the pennant. During one stretch of the season, while St. Louis was running away with the race, Bob won 15 straight games. In that winning streak he strung together 92 consecutive innings in which he gave up only one earned run. That achievement alone prompted his manager, Red Schoendienst, to proclaim, "Nobody has *ever* pitched better than Bob Gibson!"

That season the native of Omaha, Nebraska, fired 13 shutouts and tossed 28 complete games in 34 starts. He also fanned 268 batters in 305 innings. So it was no surprise when Gibson was unanimously chosen as the National League's Cy Young Award winner *and* Most Valuable Player.

Ever since 1913 the record book had contained a line that read, "Lowest Earned Run Average, 300 or more innings: 1.14." Until 1968 the owner of that record was the American League's Walter "Big Train" Johnson, probably the greatest pitcher the game has ever known. The closest any National League hurler had come to that almost unbelievable ERA was the 1.22 mark posted by the fabled Grover Cleveland Alexander in 1915. But by the time the 1968 season ended, the names of Johnson and Alexander had been replaced by that of Robert Gibson. The St. Louis star rewrote the books by limiting enemy teams to an average of 1.12 earned runs per game—slightly more than one run for every nine innings pitched!

Baseball fans all over the country were looking
forward to seeing what Gibson would do in the
upcoming Detroit–St. Louis World Series. The Tigers
were slightly favored over the Cards because of their
superior hitting. The Detroit line-up featured the bats of
Al Kaline, Willie Horton, Norm Cash, Bill Freehan and
Jim Northrup. During the regular season, Detroit hitters
had slugged 185 home runs and accumulated 640 RBI's,
while the Cardinals had produced only 73 home runs
and considerably fewer RBI's. But the Cards had some
advantages of their own: speed, a dependable defense—
and the pitching of Bob Gibson.

The St. Louis ace faced 31-game-winner Denny
McLain in the opener, played under a hot Missouri sun
before 54,692 fans. It turned out to be no contest.
McLain was knocked out of the box early in the game,
and the Cardinal right-hander mowed down Tiger after
Tiger. By shutting out the Tigers, 4–0, Gibson got his
sixth consecutive series win.

Gibson's assortment of pitches and pinpoint control
so thoroughly baffled the enemy swingers that 17 of
them went down on strikes. (Kaline and Cash each
struck out three times; Northrup, Horton and Freehan
each fanned twice.) It was a new World Series strikeout
record for a single game, surpassing by two the mark set
by Sandy Koufax in 1963. Even McLain called it "The
greatest pitching performance I've ever seen by anybody."

In game two the Tigers evened the match with an 8–1
victory, but the Cards regained their advantage with a
7–3 win in game three. The fourth game saw the second
Gibson–McLain duel. This time the Tigers reached Bob

In the 1968 World Series, Gibson fires the ball at Detroit's Norm Cash for his 16th strikeout of the day—and a new World Series record.

for one run, while the Cardinals battered McLain and several relievers for ten runs.

Gibson now had two '68 Series wins to his credit, upping his World Series career total to seven victories. With that win he set several new marks: Most Consecutive Games Won in the Series (7); Most Consecutive Complete Games Won (7); and Most Complete Games, Consecutive, in Total Series Play (8). Furthermore, Gibson had aided his own cause in that fourth game by belting out a four-bagger, his second of the Series, to become the first pitcher ever to hit more than one home run in a single World Series. He also added ten strikeouts to the 17 from his first game, bringing his two-game total to 27.

In the fifth and sixth games the Tigers bounced back with 5–3 and 13–1 victories. That brought the Series down to the seventh game. As expected, Gibson was named to start for the Cardinals. This time his opponent was Mickey Lolich, who had already won two games for Detroit.

Gibson gave it all he had, and so did Lolich. Six innings flew by, with neither side scoring. Then in the top of the seventh, with nobody on and two out, Tiger Norm Cash dropped a Texas League single into short right field. Willie Horton sent him to second with a solid single past the shortstop. Then Jim Northrup came up to bat.

Gibson checked the runners leading off first and second, wound up and unleashed a blazing fastball. Northrup connected, sending it on a line toward center field. Curt Flood, who ranks among the best outfielders in baseball, committed one of the few mistakes of his career, misjudging the ball and letting it sail over his upstretched glove. Wheeling, he caught up with the ball near the wall and fired it back to the infield. But Northrup beat the throw to third, and the two Detroit base runners scored.

Briefly dispirited by the fielding lapse, Gibson gave up another run as Bill Freehan doubled home Northrup, increasing the Tiger lead to 3–0. The weary Gibson got the third out, but yielded another run in the ninth. Meanwhile, the best the Cardinals could do against Lolich was a single run. The Tigers took the game, 3–1, and the Series, four games to three.

Flood was apologetic, and Gibson was deeply disappointed. But even in the midst of defeat the Cardinal pitcher had two shining moments. By whiffing eight Tigers in that game, he increased his strikeout total to 35—a new record for a seven-game World Series, erasing his own 1964 mark. It was also his ninth complete Series game in a row.

The next season Gibson posted a 20–13 won–lost record, struck out 269 batters and yielded only 2.18 runs per game. And 1970 provided more of the same. This time his won–lost mark was 23–7, his ERA was 3.12 and he struck out 274 batters. That was the eighth season that Bob struck out more than 200 batters, and it broke the all-time record shared by Rube Waddell and Walter Johnson. Appropriately, Gibson won the National League's Cy Young Award, for the second time in his career. He was 35 then, but still going strong.

Bob's 1971 effort was limited by still another injury (a muscle tear in his right leg), and he finished the season with a 16–13 won–lost record and a 3.04 ERA. But in 1972 the "old man" of the Cardinal mound staff came back against all the odds yet another time. Season's end saw him increase his strikeout record with another 208, giving him his ninth season of 200 or more strikeouts. And his 19–11 record and 2.46 ERA proved that he still wasn't ready for a rocking chair.

Sprinkled through the record book the name of Bob Gibson appears again and again. Sooner or later, other pitchers may come along and break one or another of his marks. But as long as his name remains, Bob Gibson will remind aspiring record-breakers that records are broken by the kind of men who never give up.

Ron Hunt

The Record that Hurt the Most

Most major-league batters achieve success by hitting the ball. Second baseman Ron Hunt believed in that method, but he added a little something extra. His idea of success also included the reverse—getting the ball to hit him! Being hit by a pitch, he figured, wasn't so bad. In fact, it was as good as a single or a walk. It got you on first base—and when you're the team's leadoff batter, that's a good place to be.

Ron did his job perfectly—and typically—in a 1973 game between his Montreal Expos and the San Francisco Giants. It was a mid-season game, held at Montreal's Jarry Park. In five times at bat, Ron reached first base five times. He rapped out three singles, drew one base on balls and was hit by a pitch. By scoring each time he got on base, he contributed five runs to the Expos' 17–3 slaughter of the Giants.

He sometimes looked funny—but Ron Hunt took his job seriously. Here he's about to slide safely home.

"That's Ron Hunt," said Montreal manager Gene Mauch. "Playing his kind of baseball. And that's a heck of a tough game to play."

Mauch's admiration for the scrappy, win-any-way style that Ron brought to each game was well earned. Ron was far from being a super-slugger. But whatever he lacked in power, he made up for with sheer determination. Getting hit was part of his everyday game plan. So were his flying slides into enemy infielders to break up double plays and his wild dashes from first to third on short singles to the outfield. His was an undying will to win that brought respect from fans and teammates alike. As Mauch told one reporter, "When a man gets on base as often as he does and fights for every extra base the way he does—you easily overlook a lack of range or a slightly slower arm. That man can play baseball!"

Ron Hunt hustled his way into a big-league line-up in 1963 when he joined the New York Mets. It was the ideal team for a player like Ron. The new expansion club featured an assortment of rejects from other teams, minor-leaguers getting the only chance they'd ever have in the majors, players who had enjoyed fine careers but were on the brink of retirement, and a few who had earned the description of "kooks." Many observers felt that Hunt fitted almost all of these categories—especially the last.

New York manager Casey Stengel once offered a $50 bonus to any player hit by a pitch with the bases loaded. No one knows how much money Hunt collected that way, but he did lead the Mets in getting hit by pitches in each of the four seasons he spent with the club. For this achievement he received Casey's rambling tribute: "It don't do you no good to get hit too many times, but it does you some good with the bases loaded because that brings in a run. Hunt could get on, which showed he had no fear and he was a game player and he was a very good man on hitting behind the runner and so on and so forth."

In his years with the Mets, 1963–66, Ron made the HBP (hit by pitch) column a total of 41 times. He did it by crowding home plate, hanging his 5-foot-10, 170-pound frame in the danger zone. He was like a man in a circus sideshow who dangles on the end of a diving board, inviting customers to drop him into the water with a well-aimed throw. The difference, of course, is that the baseballs thrown in a sideshow strike a target, and a bull's-eye trips a wire that sends the man sliding off the board. In Hunt's case, however, *he* was the target.

As a second baseman, Hunt's fielding was as reckless as his hitting. His incredible diving catches made him a favorite with Met fans—but added a few extra bruises to his battered body.

"Hunt is crazy," declared one National League pitcher who played against Ron for six years. "Any man who wants to earn his living getting ribs broken should have his head examined. The thing is, the doctors will probably find the guy's brains are already scrambled from getting hit so many times on the skull."

Nolan Ryan, whose fastball traveled close to 100 miles per hour, led the National League in hitting Hunt with pitches. It wasn't that he tried—it just happened that way. When asked for his reaction to Hunt's suicidal style of crowding the plate, Ryan said, "I think I've learned one thing about him. I can't pitch him inside."

Ryan laughed to show he was joking, but Mets' pitcher Tug McGraw was more serious when he remarked, "Hunt's unbelievable. He doesn't think about tomorrow. He can be 15 runs ahead and he's still trying to get hit or diving for a ball."

Hunt's response to critics and admirers alike was the same: to play the only way he knew how. Traded from

Trying to avoid a double play, Hunt (33) crashes into Houston shortstop Bob Lillis and sends him sprawling.

the Mets to the Los Angeles Dodgers after the 1966 season, Ron maintained his HBP average by getting in the way of pitched balls ten times in 1967. However, the Dodgers were loaded with infielders, so Hunt was traded to the San Francisco Giants. Ron made the adjustment with no noticeable change in style—running all-out, blasting into bases and fielders and daring pitchers to try to get the ball to their catchers.

From 1968 through 1970, pitchers flunked his bet-you-can't-miss-me test 76 times. Ron had now been struck by baseballs thrown by major-league hurlers on 127 different occasions. Asked why he played such a dangerous game, Ron replied: "Well, I don't have the greatest ability in the world. Far from it. I enjoy the game. I hate to lose. I'm not a dirty ballplayer. I believe in giving one hundred percent. When I play second base I make it known right away that I don't mind getting taken out with a slide and that it works both ways."

As for getting dented by curves and fastballs, he said, "It hurts. I crowd the plate and I don't give any ground and my first move is into the pitch. I hold in there that extra split second when a lot of guys are getting out of the way. If I'm going to do the job, I've got to stand there. A kid wrote and asked me if that was the easiest way to get on base. I told him, in the next game he plays, to go out and get hit by the pitch and then write me back and tell me if he thinks that's the easiest way to get on base."

The pain was part of the bargain Hunt had made to stay on a major-league roster. But he was getting older, and the skills he did have were wearing out with each passing season. When the Giants traded him to the

Hit by a pitch, Hunt is knocked to the ground. While a pinch runner went to first base, Ron was rushed to the hospital with a mild concussion.

Expos, another expansion team, he dug down deeper and came up with even more of the gutty tricks he needed to keep him going in the majors. His best trick was still the time-tested one of getting hit by pitches, which he did in a big way in 1971.

Before that season a diligent researcher had to burrow through chapters and chapters of baseball history if he wanted to unearth the record for a batter being hit by baseballs in a season. And only if he turned those pages to the pre-1900 period would he discover that Hugh A. Jennings, playing for Baltimore in the National League in 1896, was a 49-time victim of pitched balls. It took 75 years before Ronald K. Hunt revised that record, and it is written in black-and-blue ink that he encountered no fewer than 50 baseballs in the course of the season.

In addition to smashing that Golden Oldie, his total of 177 HBP's nudged him nearer to the major-league career mark of 189, set by Minnie Minoso from 1949 through 1964.

How did Ron view his achievement? "The record's not something you brag about," he admitted. "You brag about that and they'll put you in a loony house. Once someone asked me how I got hit so often. I told him I was wearing something that attracted horsehide. It was a joke, but the guy who put it in the paper didn't make it look that way. Later, one umpire wanted to search my uniform because he wanted to find what was attracting the ball."

Along with his 1971 hospital statistics, Hunt also notched 145 hits and 58 walks. That meant the man from St. Louis, Missouri, had reached base 253 times over the season, a pretty impressive contribution from a leadoff batter.

In 1972 injuries resulting from his daredevil play cut down the number of Hunt's at-bats. Still, he hung in there enough times to get plunked with 26 pitches. Minoso's mark of 189 was knocked down to second place, replaced by Hunt's grand, brand-new total of 203.

Bloodied but unbowed, 33-year-old Ron scrambled onto Jarry Park's diamond to do-or-die for his Canadian fans when the 1973 campaign began. He warmed their hearts by batting .309 for the Expos. Nevertheless, by the time the season ended, Hunt had increased his career total of HBI's to 227—a record to tempt only some future player with a death-wish greater than Ron's.

When it came to getting on base the hard way, it can truly be said that no man outbandaged Ron Hunt. If you have any doubts, just follow the suggestion of Casey Stengel, the man who witnessed many of Hunt's encounters with the pitched ball. As Casey said, "It's in the book. You could look it up."

Hoyt Wilhelm

The Supreme Reliever

The gray-haired man warming up in the Los Angeles bull pen looked like someone's grandfather getting ready for an Old-Timers' game. As he tossed the ball slowly and easily, you could imagine his arm creaking with each pitch. If he owned a fastball, he wasn't wasting his strength by throwing it now. After every pitch he glanced out at the game taking place on the field, waiting for the moment when Dodger manager Walter Alston would walk out to the mound and wave him in from the bull pen. Then old Hoyt Wilhelm would trudge to the mound and save a game.

One August night in 1972, a 6-foot, 190-pound right-hander, draped his warm-up jacket over one shoulder and went in to save another game. It was his way of life, and he loved it.

But there was something that made this game different from all the others. On this night Hoyt would be pitching for his 1,018th—and last—time in the majors. For the last time he would baffle batters with his special pitch, the knuckle ball. Not even Hoyt Wilhelm could outrun Father Time forever. At the age of 49, after 28 years in baseball (21 in the majors), he was striding out to write the last line to an amazing career.

· Hoyt Wilhelm was a 28-year-old minor-leaguer when he got his first chance in the majors with the 1952 New York Giants. Leo Durocher was the Giants' manager. The team was loaded with starting pitchers, and Durocher felt that this new hurler would have a better shot at making the staff as a reliever. Hoyt had a fair curve and fastball, but he was willing to do whatever Leo wanted. After all, he had been kicking around in the minors for seven seasons—he might not have a second chance in the big leagues.

Using Hoyt as a relief man instead of a starter was one of Durocher's wisest moves. Over the 1952 season Hoyt's efforts were all that any manager could ask for. His 2.43 earned run average was the lowest in the National League.

Hoyt stayed with the Giants through 1956, answering the call for help with steady efficiency until Durocher checked his birthdate and decided to replace him with a younger man. So the knuckle-baller joined the Cardinal bull-pen crew in St. Louis for part of a year, then moved on to the Cleveland Indians for the rest of 1957 and most of '58. Next came Baltimore where he put in four good years with the Orioles. When he joined the Orioles he was 35, an age when many pitchers begin enjoying retirement benefits. But not Hoyt Wilhelm—he was

In 1952 Giant rookie Hoyt Wilhelm demonstrates his knuckleball grip.

going as strong as ever. Given the chance to start for Baltimore, he turned in a no-hitter on September 20, 1958. As a starting pitcher the next season, Hoyt's 2.19 ERA was the best in the American League.

Wilhelm played for the Chicago White Sox uniform

from 1963 through '68. Then he headed west to the California Angels for 1969 and spent a few weeks with the Atlanta Braves before moving to the Chicago Cubs for '70. Hoyt had another short stint with the Braves before settling down with the Dodgers for 1971 and '72.

How did Wilhelm last so long and pitch so well? What was the secret of the right arm that seemed to be made of rubber? "Ain't no secret," Wilhelm said in his folksy North Carolina drawl. "When you throw the knuckler there ain't no twist on the elbow or shoulder. That's why it's easy on the arm."

Hoyt's knuckler wasn't really a knuckle ball. Like most knuckle-ballers, Hoyt used his fingertips, not his knuckles, to deliver the unpredictable pitch. As Joe Heinsen, who caught batting practice for the White Sox and Cubs when Hoyt was on their staffs, explained: "It comes off the right side of the thumb and fingernail tips of the index and middle fingers at the same instant. That way the ball has no rotation. Now the way I see it, the air pressure begins building up along the seams as the ball moves toward the plate. So the ball begins a very slow roll—maybe not even once on the entire way to home plate. But once it starts to roll, the air pressure catches the seams on another side and forces the ball to move—up, down, to either side, who knows? The reason nobody can tell which way it's going to move is that Hoyt doesn't hold it exactly the same way every time."

It dipped, it floated, it swooped, it danced. In fact, it did everything a ball could do but go in a straight line. No wonder it was nicknamed "the butterfly." A Wilhelm pitch had batters lunging one time, ducking out of the way the next. And it had catchers stabbing this way and that, digging the ball out of the dirt, smothering it on one bounce, leaping to pluck it out of the air far over their heads or way inside or outside the plate area. Most catchers used an oversized mitt just to get an even chance against the unpredictable pitch. As much as it drove catchers crazy, it was even worse for the batters who grew cross-eyed trying to track the weaving deliveries of the knuckle-ball specialist.

J. C. Martin, a catcher who handled Wilhelm's tricky tosses with the White Sox, told the story of the day Eddie Bressoud, a Red Sox shortstop, tried to solve the mystery of Hoyt's pitches. "Eddie was up to bat when Hoyt decided to start usin' the knuckler after throwin' nothin' but fastballs for five innings," Martin recalled. "Eddie, he leaped at one that went outside. Then he swung at one that went inside, and the umpire, John Rice, he called Bressoud out on the next pitch with Eddie lyin' flat on the ground."

That was the kind of misery Hoyt's dancing butterfly inflicted on batters. As for its effect on catchers, Martin had a story about that, too. "I remember in spring training," Martin drawled, "we got a cocky young catcher in camp. He talks so much about hisself we calls him Iron Jaw. He says he don't see nothin' special about catchin' this Wilhelm. He says, heck he can catch him with the regular mitt. So he gets the call to warm up ol' Hoyt, and he wears the regulation mitt and no mask. Heck, I'd never catch that guy without the big mitt and the mask. But Iron Jaw can't see it that way. Well, it's just about the time ol' Hoyt decides to test that knuckler, and he really lets loose. Iron Jaw catches one in the dirt to the right. Then he catches one to the left.

In 1968 the 45-year-old Wilhelm pitches in his 907th major-league game.

Then he gets one right in the forehead. I haven't seen him since."

Even the statisticians had trouble keeping up with the ageless relief specialist. By the time Wilhelm tied the ribbon on his career in 1972, they needed a computer to add up the totals. But when all the figures were in, the record book had some new entries. At the top was Hoyt's career total of 1,018 game appearances. Then there were the 124 games he won as a reliever. Add to that yet another major-league mark: 1,870 innings pitched in relief roles alone.

There was no one like him, this pitcher with the butterfly in his hand, who spent 21 summers rushing in from the bull pen to set the pace for all relievers to try to match. So whenever you hear people calling a new relief pitcher the greatest ever, just mention the name of Hoyt Wilhelm. Then tell them about the Old Man of the Mound, who was once described as having "a 49-year-old body, a 30-year-old arm, and a 20-year-old heart."

Cesar Gutierrez

A Perfect Day

Sunday, June 21, 1970, was a perfect day for a double-header at Cleveland's Municipal Stadium. The sun burned bright in a cloudless sky as the Indians took the field for their first game against the Detroit Tigers. But on the Tiger bench sat Venezuelan shortstop Cesar "Coco" Gutierrez, looking as darkly angry as a thundercloud. He wasn't in the starting line-up, and he grumbled to a teammate, "How can I help the team if I don't play?"

"Take it easy, Coco," the player answered. "You'll start the second game."

Gutierrez tried to smile, but as he watched his team defeat the Indians, 7–2, he became more certain he wouldn't see action in the second game either. Even though Tiger shortstop Ken Szotkiewicz didn't get a hit in three times at bat, it seemed unlikely that manager

Mayo Smith would change a winning combination. Yet when the line-up was posted for the second game, Cesar's gloom disappeared. His name was there.

The determined Gutierrez took his stance in the batter's box in the top of the first inning. To win back the job of number one shortstop, he would have to succeed with his bat as well as his glove.

Cleveland left-hander Rick Austin stared down at the small right-handed batter, reared back and fired a fastball. The 5-foot-7, 150-pound shortstop swung, and the ball leaped off the bat on a line to short-center field. His hands still tingling from the solid contact of bat against ball, Cesar pulled up at first with a single. Moments later Jim Northrup scored him from third base.

In the third inning Coco again squared off against Austin. The Indian pitcher threw a couple of curves, then tried to slip a fastball past Gutierrez. But the Detroit shortstop was ready for it, and he laced a looping drive to left field for another single. When Al Kaline followed soon after with a home run, Cesar scored his second run in the young game.

By the time Cesar came to bat in the fifth inning, Dennis Higgins had replaced Austin on the mound. On another day Gutierrez might have wished he could get another shot at a pitcher he was hitting well. But the way he felt today, it didn't matter who was throwing the ball to the plate. Cesar was in there to hit! And hit he did, slamming a knee-high curve into the hole between shortstop and third base. Shortstop Jack Heideman made a backhanded stop of the ball, but his throw was too late to beat the speedy Gutierrez.

Cesar was happy with his three-for-three performance as he waited in the on-deck circle in the seventh inning. But this was no time to let up. Cesar wasn't the only player having a good day. The Indians were also scoring runs in a game that had become a hitter's battle.

"Get another one, Coco," a young fan yelled from the stands.

The 27-year-old Tiger nodded in the direction of the youngster, then stepped in to face Dennis Higgins for the second time that afternoon. The Cleveland hurler's first pitch was outside, and Cesar let it go by. The second pitch was tight, forcing him to jump back. The next one was inside but on the corner, and Cesar lashed at it, driving the ball past the glove of the diving third baseman. Gutierrez sped to first, stumbled briefly, kept his balance and headed for second. He reached it standing up, well ahead of the left fielder's throw. That was all the hard running he had to do for the rest of the inning. When Detroit outfielder Jim Northrup collected his second four-bagger, Coco just trotted home to score his third run of the game.

In the eighth inning Coco made his fifth appearance at the plate. Mickey Stanley was on first, Gates Brown was on third and the Tigers were behind, 8–7. It was a clutch situation, and Cesar was glad that the manager hadn't decided to pinch-hit for him.

Gutierrez was looking for a curve on the first pitch, but he got a fastball. Coco swung and missed. He stepped out of the batter's box, scooped up some dirt and rubbed it onto his sweat-slick palms. As he did so, he glanced down at the third-base coach, who gave the signal to hit away.

Detroit's Cesar Gutierrez had plenty to smile about on June 21, 1970.

Digging in, Cesar gripped the bat tightly and eyed the pitcher. The ball came in, a curve, and he jumped at it, sending a line drive over the head of second baseman Eddie Leon. Gates Brown dashed across home plate with the tying run as Cesar pulled up at first.

No more runs scored in the eighth inning or the ninth, and the game went into extra innings. In the tenth Coco came to bat with one out and Don Wert on first base. Indian reliever Phil Hennigan bore down hard in an effort to cool off Cesar's hot bat. But he couldn't stop Gutierrez, who slashed the ball just past the mound. As it bounced over second base the Indian shortstop made a desperate lunge and knocked it down with his glove. He picked up the ball and flipped it to the second baseman, hoping to force Wert. But the throw was too late. Wert was safe at second and Gutierrez was perched on first with hit number six to his credit.

Both clubs failed to break the tie through the tenth and eleventh innings. In the top of the twelfth, however, Mickey Stanley put Detroit ahead by hammering a homer off Hennigan. The Cleveland fans groaned—this could mean the loss of a doubleheader—but they couldn't help cheering when they saw the next Detroit batter step in to hit.

It was Cesar Gutierrez, on the edge of baseball immortality. One more hit and he would set a standard that had eluded even the greatest baseball sluggers. Not since 1892 had anyone gotten seven hits in a row in a single game. Since then several players had gone six-for-six, including the incomparable Ty Cobb back in 1925, but never seven-for-seven.

Hennigan wound up and blazed the ball toward his catcher, but it never reached the waiting mitt. Cesar's bat came around and drove the ball back at the pitcher's feet. As Hennigan tried to spear it, the ball bounced off his glove and trickled away. By the time he got to it and threw to first, the umpire's hands were stretched flat out in the "Safe!" signal.

Seven-for-seven, six singles and a double—the high point in the baseball career of Cesar Gutierrez. When that season ended, Gutierrez's batting average was an unimpressive .243, and not too long afterward he was out of the majors. But he finished his career knowing that it would be a long time before his record would be broken.

Tom Seaver

The 10-K Streak of Tom Terrific

Pitching for the New York Mets in their early years was as frustrating as trying to swim in glue. You gave up three runs, and you lost. Allowed only two runs, and lost. Held the opposition to a single run, and lost. Knowing he had to hurl with that kind of non-support, a pitcher could lose heart in a hurry. Only one with plenty of heart—and plenty of stuff on his pitches—could be a winner with such a team. In other words, a Tom Seaver.

When Tom joined the Mets' mound staff in 1967, the Shea Stadium team was the laughingstock of the National League. They struggled through that season and finished dead last, winning a mere 61 games against a walloping 101 losses. But no one could laugh at Seaver or his impressive 16–13 record. The new Met struck out 170 batters and had a 2.76 earned run average. How can

Met ace Tom Seaver throws the ball straight past the camera.

you laugh at a man who's voted Rookie of the Year? Not even the Mets could keep Seaver down. In 1968 the New Yorkers wound up just one game out of last place, and their club batting average was the lowest in the league. This time they won 73 games and lost 89. Nevertheless, Seaver won 16, lost 12, and fanned 205 batters. His 2.20 ERA was seventh best in the league.

Then something happened in 1969 that has to be regarded as one of the fairy tales of modern-day baseball. In one incredible season those lovable clowns leaped from the bottom of the league to the top of the world. They not only captured the pennant, but amazed the entire sports world by defeating the Baltimore Orioles in five games for the World Series crown.

The Mets' hitting was still weak in 1969, but their pitching more than made up for it. Supplying the spark all season long and coming up with the big wins, Seaver won 25 and lost just 7. He struck out 208 men, and his 2.21 ERA was fourth best in the league. He was the champion of champions and, fittingly, was named the National League's Cy Young Award winner. He also earned the 1969 Hickock Belt as the outstanding professional athlete in the United States.

The fortunes of the Mets returned to normal in 1970. The New Yorkers could do no better than third place in the six-team Eastern half of the NL. Was Seaver to blame? Not by any stretch of the imagination! While the Mets were posting an 83–79 record, the man now being referred to as "Tom Terrific" won 18 and lost 12. He also struck out 283 batters and maintained a 2.81 ERA—the best in the league.

Tom Terrific really earned his nickname on April 22,

1970. The Mets were playing the San Diego Padres at Shea Stadium. The first five innings were fairly uneventful. The Padres picked up a run on Al Ferrara's homer, while Tom's teammates scratched out two runs in his behalf. The only other interesting fact was that Seaver had struck out nine Padres by the time he faced Ferrara with two out in the sixth. Yet his catcher, Jerry Grote, wasn't particularly impressed at that moment. "Actually," Grote said after the game, "he wasn't very strong in the early innings. He just kept building as the game went on."

The "building up" started when Tom notched his tenth strikeout by retiring Ferrara on a fastball to end the sixth inning. Then Seaver really caught fire. To open the seventh, he arched a hairpin curve past Nate Colbert's swinging bat for strike three. Dave Campbell took a called third strike, and Jerry Morales followed his example, giving Seaver the pleasure of fanning the side in order.

In the eighth inning Bob Barton was San Diego's first batter. Barton was also Tom's first strikeout of the inning, as he went down on a called third strike. Pinch-hitter Ramon Webster changed the pattern a trifle—by swinging at—but missing—a third strike. That gave Seaver 15 strikeouts for the game, tying him for the Mets' club record with Nolan Ryan, who had set the mark just five days earlier. Tom swiftly passed Ryan's high by whiffing another pinch-hitter, Ivan Murrell, for his 16th strikeout of the game, and the seventh in a row.

As the ninth inning got underway the score was still 2–1. It could have been 200–1 as far as the 14,197 fans

Tom shows the concentration that helped him strike out ten men in a row.

were concerned. Seaver was creating a mound master-piece, and his non-stop run of strikeouts was all that really mattered to them.

In the thousands of big-league games played before this one, only four pitchers had ever fanned eight batters in a row. Seaver joined them by disposing of Van Kelly with three pitches to open the ninth. He left their company one batter later by blowing three pitches past Clarence Gaston, who watched the third one go by without even moving the bat from his shoulder. Nine in a row was a new record. But now Seaver had also struck out 18 in the game. Could he strike out the last batter to make it ten in a row and tie Steve Carlton's record of 19 for one game?

But Seaver's attention was as much on the game as on records as he faced Al Ferrara, the third batter in the ninth. "I kept thinking about Ferrara and the fact that he hit a home run off me earlier," Tom said later. "I was just afraid I might make a mistake on him."

There was no mistake on the first pitch, a slider that nipped the outside corner. "Strike one!" called plate umpire Harry Wendelstedt. Ferrara shook his head and got set for the next pitch. "Ball one," Wendelstedt said, and the crowd booed. The count jumped to 1–and–2 as the next pitch, a fastball, drilled into Grote's mitt, untouched by the ferocious cut taken by the batter.

The Mets' right-hander looked cool standing in the middle of the diamond, rubbing the ball in his hands. But he was thinking hard. "I may never come this close again. I might as well go for it," he may have told himself. "I'm going to challenge him with a fastball!"

The 6-foot-1 hurler began his motion, came to a stop

with his hands at belt level, and got ready to put every ounce of his 200 pounds behind the pitch . . .

Meanwhile Ferrara was having some thoughts of his own. "I knew he was going to give me his heat," the San Diego player told reporters afterward, "because he was really bringing it in. It was *his* best shot against *my* best shot."

Seaver's shot was better. "Strike three! You're out!" the umpire yelled.

With that last lightning pitch, the Met ace had tied one major-league record and set another. The one he set, on his tenth successive strikeout, was a feat that had escaped such speedballers as Sandy Koufax, Walter Johnson, Bob Feller, Sam McDowell, Dizzy Dean, Lefty Grove and Christy Mathewson. None of them had even come close to Seaver's ten in a row.

Ed Kranepool, the Mets' first baseman, was thrilled to be part of the record-breaker. "Tom was like a machine those last few innings," he raved. "Whomp, whomp, whomp! Fastballs, sliders, curves! Wow!"

Johnny Podres, a former Brooklyn Dodger who was one of the four pitchers to hold the record of eight straight strikeouts, was another impressed witness. "He was fantastic. Outstanding," Podres said. "As hard as he was throwing, he was still hitting the spots. If you didn't swing, it was still a strike."

Umpire Harry Wendelstedt and Met catcher Jerry Grote had the clearest views of anyone in the park. To Wendelstedt it looked like "one heck of a fastball. It was zip, zip, zip." And Grote, who made the record books himself by handling 20 put-outs in a nine-inning game, said, "Now you know why Tom's terrific."

And then there were Tom's 19 strikeouts. That total tied the major-league mark set by Steve Carlton, who had struck out 19 Mets just one year earlier. Ironically, Carlton had lost that game to these same weak-hitting New Yorkers.

When asked to compare Carlton's 19-strikeout performance to Seaver's, Met pitching coach Rube Walker said, "I'll tell you something—when Carlton struck out 19 of us last year, I said that no one would match that

Seaver's right knee almost touches the ground as he fires another strike past the batter.

record for a long time. Well, sonofagun, if this guy doesn't come along and match it within one season. But I'll stake a lot on this prediction: I don't think anyone's going to come along for a long, long time and match those ten strikeouts in a row."

What could Seaver do in 1971 that would even mildly approach his 1970 effort? Nothing stupendous, as it turned out—just win 20 games against 10 losses and break his own record for strikeouts by a right-hander, with 289. Without him, the Mets would have been close to the cellar instead of finishing in a tie for third place. Toiling for a no-hit club, he deserved a special medal for racking up 20 wins. Instead, he received something just as good—recognition for turning in the lowest earned run average—1.76—in the majors for 1971. It was his second straight year as the league's ERA king.

Racing along at his Hall-of-Fame rate, Tom logged another fine season in 1972, with a 2.92 ERA and 249 strikeouts. Along with those figures went a 21–12 won–lost record.

In 1973 the Mets pulled off another miracle. Late in August they were last in their division; but a great September surge—and some super-Seaver pitching—carried them all the way to the World Series. The Mets finally bowed to Oakland in a seven-game cliff-hanger, but Tom's outstanding effort earned him his second Cy Young award.

But not even a world championship has the stature to equal the peak of personal triumph Tom scaled on that record-shattering April day in 1970. Ten consecutive strikeouts, 19 in all. As Jerry Grote said, "Now you know why Tom's terrific!"

Willie Mays

Off the Record

Baseball's record books don't have a category called "Greatest Fielding Plays, Lifetime." Such plays can't be broken down into numbers or measured by distance. Like miracles, they simply happen. And when they do, baseball fans *know* that they're seeing something extraordinary.

On September 29, 1954, more than 52,000 fans in New York's old Polo Grounds witnessed a truly miraculous feat. It was the opening game of that year's World Series between the New York Giants and the Cleveland Indians. The score was tied 2–2 in the top of the eighth. The Indians were on the warpath, threatening to break the game open. With Cleveland runners on first and second, slugger Vic Wertz came to bat. Giant Willie Mays was patroling center field—and it was the biggest center field in baseball, with fences averaging 450 feet from home plate. Wertz was 3–for–3 for the afternoon, and since he had tripled down the right-field alley his first time up, Mays moved over toward right.

Giant pitcher Don Liddle reared back and threw. Wertz's bat blurred, there was a sharp *crack*, and the baseball blasted off toward center field. It was headed for the deepest part of the Polo Grounds.

As bat met ball, Mays took off. Whirling and sprinting at full speed, he raced toward the bleacher wall. The ball was zooming and so was Mays. Still going all-out, his back to the plate, Willie reached the warning track a few feet from the wall. Then, as if an alarm had rung to tell him now was the perfect time to turn, he looked over his left shoulder and snared the ball just before it—and he—reached the wall, 460 feet from the plate. In any other ballpark Wertz's drive would have been a home run. And against any other fielder it would have been a two-run double. But against Willie Mays in the Polo Grounds, it was a long, spectacular out.

Digging his spikes into the cinders, Mays braked to a stop, spun and gunned the ball on a line to second baseman Davey Williams. The Cleveland runners, stunned by Willie's catch, barely got back to their bases.

New York went on to win the game, 5–2, in the tenth inning. It was a game that would surely have ended after nine innings—with Cleveland on top—if not for the fantastic fielding of Willie Howard Mays. "The Catch," as it came to be known, had an effect on both teams. It took the heart right out of the Indians—and put heart into the Giants. Confident that no team on earth could beat them after a play like that, the New Yorkers ran away with the Series in four straight.

Willie Mays is about to make the most famous catch in baseball history.

It was Willie Mays' second full season as a major-leaguer and his first as a World Series player. He had already won Rookie of the Year honors in 1951, but after the 1954 season and Series, he was declared the Most Valuable Player in the National League, Major League Player of the Year, Male Athlete of the Year and Professional Athlete of the Year. He earned those awards with his fielding, his uncanny base-running and his bat. With that bat, Mays had socked 41 home runs, driven in 110 runs and led the National League with a .345 batting average. But "The Catch" sparkled brighter than every other achievement that year.

As graceful and daring as he was strong, 5-foot-11, 190-pound Willie Mays was the most exciting ballplayer the sport had ever known. His enthusiasm for the game was unlimited, and it bubbled up so readily that he was quickly dubbed the "Say-Hey Kid." The "Say-Hey" part came from the expression he used to show his surprise or delight at something that was said or happened. The "Kid" part was a natural, because that was what the young Giant was like—a kid who seemed to be playing ball on some sandlot or city street rather than in a big-league stadium.

But for all his boyish enthusiasm, Mays was all business with a glove or a bat. And a major part of his business was hitting home runs. In 1955 he smashed out a league-leading 51 homers. He repeated his home-run leadership in 1962 with 49, in '64 with 47, and in '65 with 52. The 660 four-baggers he hit between 1951 and 1973 made him the third highest home-run hitter of all time. Only Babe Ruth and Hank Aaron were ahead of him on the list.

In 1972, after 21 years in a Giant uniform in New York and San Francisco, Willie was sold to the New York Mets. Although the 40-year-old center fielder was still a better ballplayer than most major-leaguers half his age, many of his friends and fans began to wish he would retire. "Willie is just as thrilling to watch as he ever was," a New York sportswriter said at the end of the 1972 season, "but he just can't perform at the level that made him the finest player I've seen in the past 30 years. He's fading, and it's a sad thing to see."

Willie hit only eight homers in 1972. And his bat was even weaker in 1973. Not only did his homer output skid to six, but his season average dipped to .211, far below his lifetime batting mark of .303.

Yet just a few years earlier in 1969, the Baseball Writers' Association poll had named Mays to their team of baseball's greatest living players. At that time former Giant manager Leo Durocher said: "Mays could pick up a team and carry it on his back. Maybe it was a hit, maybe it was a catch, maybe it was the way he ran the bases. Every day he came to play. Every day he'd do the unexpected."

"But Leo," a sportscaster said, "you're talking about Willie when he was in his 20s."

"I know that," Durocher answered, "but he still can do it all whenever he wants. Even today, this minute, he's more exciting than anybody who ever played this game."

A good portion of that excitement was exhibited in All-Star games. Willie made the All-Star line-up for the first time in 1954, and he was a permanent member from then on. Appearing in those showcase contests for

After 21 years in a Giant uniform, Mays returned to New York as a Met.

20 years, Mays left his stamp on every game as a dangerous base runner, a no-fault fielder and a super-slugger. Along the way he recorded the most career hits in All-Star play (23), most stolen bases (6) and most runs scored (20). He also tied Stan Musial for most extra-base hits (8), and most total bases (40). In addition, he finished in a flat-footed tie with Brooks Robinson in the triples department; each rapped out three in All-Star competition.

Along with those All-Star marks, Willie left behind two other records unmatched by any other National League player. One was his career accumulation of runs scored, which had soared to 2,038 by the end of 1972. Every run he scored thereafter made it just that much harder for anyone ever to catch up with him.

His second NL record, however, was one he would have been glad to see erased by someone else. It was the total of 1,526 strikeouts he amassed through 1973. They were nothing to brag about, of course, but they did put him in the company of such other strikeout kings as Babe Ruth, Mickey Mantle, Harmon Killebrew and Dick Allen.

Throughout his magnificent career Willie had so many great days and great seasons that it seemed impossible to pick out one time when his bat was at its best. So we turned to Mays himself to select his favorite hitting performance, and he spun the clock back to April 30, 1961.

On that memorable afternoon, Willie completely mangled the Milwaukee Braves' pitching. In the first inning, with the bases empty, he whacked a home run off Lew Burdette. He slammed another one off Burdette

A day to remember: Mays hits his fourth homer of the game on May 4, 1961.

in the third, with one man on. Two Giants were waiting to score in the sixth when Willie brought them in by bashing a Seth Morehead pitch for a three-run homer. When Willie came up again in the eighth, Don McMahon was on the mound for Milwaukee, and the Giants had one man on base. A few moments later Willie was denting home plate after circling the bases for home run number four. That run also gave him eight RBI's for the day. The quartet of four-baggers tied him with eight other major-leaguers who hit that many in one game. "It was the greatest day I ever had," Willie declared.

That day must have been in Willie's mind on September 20, 1973. Saying, "It's time to quit when you're 42 and hitting .211," Mays announced that the '73 season would be his last in active baseball.

All good things must come to an end, and the glorious 22-year career of Willie Mays was no exception. His home runs and stolen bases are on the record books for all to see. But for Mays, these were only two of his weapons. Two others—magnificent fielding and enthusiasm—are off the record, but will one day help send the "Say-Hey Kid" to baseball's Hall of Fame. "Say hey!"

Index

Page numbers in italics refer to photographs.